Grown-Up Children Grown-Up Parents

*Opening the Door to Healthy
Relationships Between Parents
and Adult Children*

Phyllis Lieber, Gloria S. Murphy,
and Annette Merkur Schwartz

A Birch Lane Press Book
Published by Carol Publishing Group

A Birch Lane Press Book
Published by Carol Publishing Group
Birch Lane is a registered trademark of Carol Communications, Inc.
Editorial Offices: 600 Madison Avenue, New York, N.Y. 10022
Sales and Distribution Offices: 120 Enterprise Avenue, Secaucus, N.J. 07094
In Canada: Canadian Manda Group, P.O. Box 920, Station U, Toronto, Ontario
   M8Z 5P9
Queries regarding rights and permissions should be addressed to Carol Publishing
Group, 600 Madison Avenue, New York, N.Y. 10022

Carol Publishing Group books are available at special discounts for bulk
purchases, sales promotions, fund-raising, or educational purposes.
Special editions can be created to specifications. For details, contact Special
Sales Department, Carol Publishing Group, 120 Enterprise Avenue, Secaucus,
N.J. 07094

Manufactured in the United States of America
10 9 8 7 6 5 4 3 2 1

Library of Congress Cataloging-in-Publication Data

Lieber, Phyllis.
   Grown-up children, grown-up parents : opening the door to healthy
   relationships between parents and adult children / by Phyllis
   Lieber, Gloria S. Murphy, and Annette Merkur Schwartz.
        p.   cm.
   "A Birch Lane Press book."
   ISBN 1-55972-243-6
   1. Parent and adult child.   I. Murphy, Gloria S.   II. Schwartz,
Annette Merkur.   III. Title.
HQ755.86.L54   1994
306.874—dc20   94-16678
                                                        CIP

To our dear husbands
Ed, Phil, and the memory of Sidney, who lovingly shared
with us the role of parenting

Contents

Acknowledgments

We acknowledge with gratitude, the following people who contributed to the creation of this project:

Lillian Perlick, for her contribution to the early preparation of the book; Bernard Stebel, our attorney and friend, who has long counseled and encouraged us; Stephen Gelfman, for his legal contribution; Murray Benson, who continuously supported us with his knowledge of the publishing field; Connie Clausen, for her contribution in moving our project forward; Taffy Gould McCallum, for her support, and for the opportunity to be interviewed on her talk show; Milton (Mitch) Lipson, who generously gave us the benefit of his clear thinking; Virginia Sullivan, for her kindness in consulting with us about some of our early writing; Dvera Berson, who shared her experiences in having her books published; Ward Botsford, for his interest and suggestions; and Alvin Arnold, for his professional advice.

We thank our editors, Eileen Cotton and Jim Ellison, for their encouragement and editorial management.

With hearts full of love, we thank our children who contributed their professional judgement and practical advice:

Steven and Ann Pleshette Murphy, Jeanne Murphy and Bill Oris, Lois Murphy and Ben Eisner, Kevin and Miriam Murphy; Myra Lieber and Michael Natter, Anne Lieber and Robert Silverman; Leslie Schwartz and Ching Wan Tang, Melissa Schwartz and Aftab Omer.

Special appreciation goes to Phyllis's mother, Evelyn Paull, who adopted our philosophy of parenting as the book was being written.

We thank our many friends and other family members for their unwavering and loving support:

Barbara and Steven Lind, Joanne and Eddie Faber, Arlene and Leon Fuhrman, Claudette and Sid Caplin, Doris Benson, and the "Camelot Group."

Grown-Up Children, Grown-Up Parents

Introduction

Parents of adult children wonder:

"What is my role now that my child is grown? Is my job finished? I feel as if I'm on stage without a script."

When the children were small, we kept on the night table, close at hand, a guidebook on child care. Now we need information on how to relate to young adults.

Changing social times have caused a revolution in family dynamics, opening up a Pandora's box of problems. What are parents worrying about today?

- Many young people have dramatically different lifestyles from those of their parents.
- Young people are remaining single longer, and are delaying parenthood until they are in their thirties.
- There is increased incidence of divorce among all ages.
- More grown children are returning to the nest.

The problems may not be new, but the approaches taken for solving them should be in keeping with the changing social times. The goals remain the same—to be happy with who *we* are, accept who *they* are, and give each other mutual respect.

This book teaches practical methods for forming satisfying

relationships with your adult children, while keeping a focus on your own pursuits.

There are two ways to use this book. Read it from start to finish to gain new insights into this stage of your life. Use it as a handbook, thumbing through the pages, to identify those circumstances that mirror events happening around you. You will find pertinent information, vignettes of people in various situations, and reflective exercises that help you practice or review what you have learned.

You will come across a variety of topics:

- Redefining the parental role
- Acknowledging growth changes in ourselves
- Reducing the child's dependency on the parent and the parent's dependency on the child
- Setting aside "what if" and accepting "what is"
- Confronting the fear of loss of the old relationship
- Creating a new appropriate bond

Reading about other people—whether their situations are similar to yours or those of people you know—will help you gain understanding about your own circumstances.

The most assured, competent parents are often perplexed and upset by their adult children's behavior.

"My son lost his job some time ago and has had a hard time finding something else in his field. For two months now, he and his wife and their children have been living with us. We love them, and want to help out, but our house and our lives have been completely disrupted. Our grandchildren romp all over the house. The TV is always on. The telephone rings constantly. The refrigerator door never closes.

"How can we be helpful to our children and still maintain a lifestyle of our own?"

"My daughter is planning to go back to work when our grandson is only three months old. I stayed home with every one of my children, because there's no substitute for mother love. Of course, every time I tell her what I think, she gets angry.

"Do I have to keep my opinions to myself?"

"My daughter is twenty-five, and she still asks us for money to keep her head above water. I feel guilty if I think about saying 'no,' and I feel foolish to keep saying 'yes.'

"Is there a way to free her—and ourselves—from the dependency?"

As parents of adult children we share a similar goal: to create a loving, caring relationship with our adult children without dependence or domination. At the same time we can rejoice in our newfound freedom and enjoy this new stage in our lives.

Chapter 1

Letting Go

When do we stop being parents? Never. When do we start being *different* kinds of parents, backing off from our earlier attachments, treating our children as adults? That timetable depends on how we raised them, what our expectations were, and what they are now. The idea of thinking of one's child as an adult is an unfamiliar one to some parents. They still consider their children as they "always were"—either frozen in some far-off charming memory, or constantly in need of direction.

Audrey's husband was sitting in front of the television set, engrossed in watching his favorite baseball team. Suddenly, his view was blocked by Audrey standing directly in front of him.

"Imagine. Caroline finally finishes the loan for all that furniture and off she goes on a cruise—a *luxury* cruise. When she gets back I'm going to have to tell her that she's spending money wildly, without any concern for the future."

"I thought we'd let go of that kind of interference five years ago," said her husband, moving his head so he could see the game.

Audrey told us that she knew her husband was right. "I guess I've still got a lot to learn," she said.

There we have it, the essence of dealing with our grown children: LETTING GO—learning to relinquish the old strings. Recognizing, acknowledging, and accepting the fact that although they are, and always will be, our children, they are now adults with lives of their own.

Separating: Beginning to Let Go

Methods of parenting have always been in dispute. If we're too nurturing, we're overprotective; too sheltering, we're smothering; too directive, we're controlling; too acquiescent, we're permissive—inept, lazy, not doing our job. "Cut the cord as soon as possible," was popular advice a couple of decades ago. "Teach your child to walk—and to walk away." Such advice describes the parents' role as purely custodial. Give birth to the child, see him through his school years, and then say, "So long, kid."

For many people the reality is closer to "once a parent, always a parent." But we do not want to stay "stuck" in the earlier stages of parenthood. When our children become adults, a new, more appropriate stage of parenting is needed. Instead of cutting the cord or ripping it apart—or keeping our children inexorably tangled in it—we can stretch it with a gradual and loving process called "letting go."

Audrey, who was worried about the way her daughter was spending money, took the first step to letting go by acknowledging that she still had a road ahead of her. Awareness and acknowledgment come first.

The process of letting go requires that we:

- Become aware that some form of separation is inevitable and necessary.
- Acknowledge our own grieving period over the loss of our "job" as parents of young, dependent children.
- Redefine our parental role.
- Be willing to let go of always "running the show."
- Be willing to share the role of "master of ceremonies."

Those parents who identify themselves mainly as parents have a harder time letting go of their adult children than do those who have had active, other-directed lives throughout their children's growing up. Some fathers have an easier time than mothers do because traditionally a man's main emphasis was on his career, whereas a mother's main emphasis was on her children. These old patterns have undergone drastic changes in the last ten or fifteen years.

When we acknowledge and accept the *separateness* of our grown children, we then have the opportunity to express and expand our own individuality. We can now establish priorities for ourselves and direct our energies toward new (or old!) interests and activities. Being parents of adults permits us to focus on personal endeavors, while keeping a wholesome balance in the family relationship.

Letting go, separating, is an ongoing process. A child does not one day announce, "I am separating." Neither does the parent. Separating can start during adolescence or long after, and may be perceived by the parent as rebelliousness, rejection, or withdrawal.

Life does not progress on a steady path. There are stops and starts and regressions. We sometimes are surprised when our children revert to behavior that made us uncomfortable when they were teenagers. For example, a father was startled by his son's outburst of anger toward him over a disagreement about a sports event. He was reminded of an incident that occurred during his son's adolescence. He recalled what he had said at the time. "I know you're trying to cut the cord, but must you insist upon using a rusty old saw?"

Another parent described an ordeal she and her husband had recently endured.

"All weekend we waited for Robert to call," said Estelle. "We didn't get a wink of sleep. Was he in a car accident? Did his friend's house burn down? Was he lying somewhere in a coma?"

Robert is not a ten-year-old child, visiting a schoolmate. He is twenty-five, a third-year graduate student who had driven to another city to visit his girlfriend. To the outside world, he is an adult. But he is still his parents' child, and they still worry when he goes off to another city. We might conclude that he is thoughtless and spoiled—unless ... Unless his parents have always been overprotective and interfering and this is his way of showing independence. Or his parents disapprove of his girlfriend and this is his way of making a statement. Or his parents like his girlfriend but disapprove of his spending a weekend with her. Another statement.

Or we might conclude that Robert is being rebellious, that he is separating, not because of the weekend trip itself, but by not calling his parents to reassure them that he had arrived safely.

Afterward, Estelle and her husband faced a dilemma. They did not wish to yell or scold, nor did they wish to inflict guilt on their son. They decided to use a light touch.

"You know us, Rob," Estelle told her son. "Visions of hurricanes, tornadoes, and earthquakes are always lurking in our brains.

"You're an adult, a responsible one—we don't question that. We question the way the world works. How can we *not* worry? Just give us a ring next time so we'll know you got there safely."

Thus, Estelle and her husband revealed their feelings, while they reaffirmed their confidence in their son. There may come a time when they will not need that reassuring call, when they will assume that he is fine. Meanwhile, Robert will understand their fears and will not feel that he is being unduly fussed over.

How much of our children's actions do we interpret correctly? How much of what we hear our children say is authentic? How much do we change because of our own egos?

Parent *says*: "Call me if you need me."
Child *says*: "Oh, I won't need to call you."
Parent *hears:* "I don't need you."

How willing are we to give up being needed all the time? Is there a demarcation, a specific point when a parent no longer says, "Call us the minute you arrive"? When your children pursue what you consider the wrong careers or lifestyles, or choose the wrong friends or spouses, what are you supposed to do—smile and tell them everything's fine, stay on the sidelines and say nothing, look on with pointing fingers and disapproving eyes, or reveal your true opinions?

The Parents' Role: New and Changing

A parent plays a major role in the separation process. If you did not give your children increasing levels of responsibility and independence during their adolescence, do not despair. You can give it to them now—by not wanting to know every detail of their lives, by assuring them that they are not deserting you when they move out, and by not rushing to rescue them from every flat tire or every overdue bill. Learn to recognize your child's moves to separate; learn to respond appropriately—or bite your tongue! Do not wait for your child to make all the moves.

How eager are we to reduce our children's dependency? Do we mourn for the pretty pink picture of the past when the children were small, safe in a warm cocoon *we* created? Do we try to negate the present by falling into the "if only" trap?

- If only the children didn't live so far away.
- If only the oldest would get married.
- If only the middle one would get out of show business.
- If only the "baby" hadn't married so young.
- If only, if only . . .

Do we then turn the spotlight on ourselves?

- If only we had given the children more religion—or less religion.
- If only we had sent them to a commuting college—or an out-of-state college.
- If only we had encouraged them to get jobs while they were teenagers—or not let them work and become independent so early.
- If only, if only . . .

To combat falling into the "if only" trap, a parent needs an acrobatic memory that does high jumps way out of sight and then snaps back with ease when the photo album gets pulled down from the shelf.

We have to be a little selective with our memories and realize that they are fragile treasures. Remembering past years is fine, but remembering with endless regret indicates that we have not completed our early role of parenting. Such wishful thinking leads nowhere.

We can all think back to when our children were little and be honest in acknowledging that we made some mistakes. We may be tempted to use the "if only" excuse: "If only I could do it over—I would do it differently."

Is this simply hindsight—which softens recollections and blurs the edges of memory? Is our current judgment formed and colored by the knowledge of how things are today in a rapidly changing world? Does our change in thought reflect the easing of our expectations and the changes in ways of living today? The answer to these questions is most likely "yes." Yes, we are speaking from hindsight; we cannot help but be influenced in this new way of thinking by all that has happened since our children were little.

There are questions we can address at the present time:

- What is happening *now*?
- Who are our children *now*?

And there are methods of behavior we can employ:

- Forget about past role playing and past behavior.
- Tackle each situation as it happens, without an old script attached.

Years ago, there was the caricature of adult children tied to their parents' apron strings, completely at the parents' beck and call. An extreme example of this was the family of the poet Elizabeth Barrett Browning, whose father dominated eleven adult sons and daughters, forcing them to live at home.

Such a situation seems ludicrous today. But figurative apron strings still exist; some parents or children are unwilling or unable to untie them. Some parents create a climate of supervision by constantly overseeing and monitoring their children's behavior and activities, if even just in their own minds.

The now classic joke about the inability of both parent and child to let go illustrates the strength of the bond between them:

Mother picked up the ringing phone.
"Hello."
"Ma?"
"What's wrong, what happened?"
"The baby cried all night—I have a migraine—six people are coming for dinner—and I forgot to buy coffee."
"My poor darling. How's the baby now?"
"Sleeping. Oh, Ma, what'll I do?"
"I'll be right over. You'll lie down with a cold compress. I'll take care of the baby. I'll prepare dinner. I'll set the table. And I'll bring a can of coffee."
"Oh, Ma, thank you. And Don will thank you, too."
"Don? But your husband's name is Joe."
"No, Ma, his name is Don. Is this—789-1234?"
"No, this is 789-1235. You must have dialed the wrong number."
"Oh. Does this—does this mean you're not coming?"

An old joke, a familiar story, but one to which we can all relate. It is a parent's natural inclination to respond to the plea of a child, even an adult child. But "once a parent always a parent, once a child always a child" is too simplistic a statement. Nothing stays the same. This does not mean that a mother should refuse to help her daughter, or that a daughter should not seek help from her mother. Moderation is the key here. The degree and frequency of dependency influence the relationship. We have to redefine for ourselves the parental role. How much do we give; how much do we take?

What kind of relationship do we want with our children? "Finish your string beans," says the mother. She does not see Bill, the football quarterback, or Bill, the husband and father; she sees Billy, the skinny little boy of twenty years ago. Moreover she sees herself in her old role of busy young mother.

Telling one's grown son to eat his vegetables may be valid in some relationships, but not in others. It depends on the tone of voice used, the choice of words, how many times the words are repeated, what went on before the telling years before, and how the parent treats the child generally. If we behave toward our children with respect—the same kind of respect we give to strangers—we will gain closeness and rapport. Then, telling them to finish their vegetables can fit in with that closeness.

What of the children? How eager are they to reduce the dependency? Constantly rescuing them sends out the message that you are the parent—the rescuer, the protector—and they are the children, dependent and helpless. Such a message is rooted in fantasy. It stunts your children's growth, and it stunts yours as well.

Parents want to feel proud of their children's choices, decisions, and achievements, but how can the children accomplish anything if parents are always doing things for them?

Children have to *feel* grown-up, or they won't *act* grown-up. Parents play the prelude in their children's lives; it is the children's role to play the main piece.

If you feel that your adult children are too clinging, throw in a little benign neglect, at the same time keeping the conversation upbeat and cheerful:

- "I understand, and I do sympathize."
- "I wish I could help you, but right now I can't."
- "I have every confidence that you'll work it out."

By giving your children the opportunities, and the "space," to run their own lives; by listening to them with sympathy, understanding, and respect; and by telling them, "I have every confidence that you'll work it out," you are implying not only that they will solve their problems, but also that they will do it *themselves*, and in a satisfactory way.

When you speak with sincere concern, you show your children that they are not being rejected. You don't have to be available all the time—physically, that is. You can always be available in spirit: "Oh, we'd love to take the baby for the weekend, but we've got the camera club outing. But next weekend would be great." Not a refusal and not merely a postponement, this reply encompasses love, eagerness, *and* the fact that you have your own activities. It can serve as a mutual declaration of independence.

The Art of Interacting: The Start
of a Changing Relationship

The family structure has changed, but the ideal concept of a loving, caring, *special* entity, without dependence or domination on the part of its members, can be preserved—or created. Indeed, it can flourish—and so can we.

As with any human interaction, at the center of our new relationship with our children is communication. How we communicate with each other determines the nature of the relationship. Communication between the generations calls for understanding, thought, and planning. Listening—really listening—as our children speak, commenting without negative criticism or evaluation, and contributing a wide range of interesting topics to family conversations will all help promote closeness.

Remember when the children came home from kindergarten? "What did you do today?" you asked. One child would give a complete rundown; the other would clam up, or simply say, "Nothing." Even for children who liked to give full descriptions of their activities, this was the beginning of their awareness that they owned a bit of life apart from their parents.

Now, more than ever, the need for privacy for your adult child and for yourself is crucial to your new role. When you respect your own privacy, you will be better able to respect the privacy of your children.

Some parents want to know all about their children's lives; some reveal everything about their own lives.

Tessa fell into both categories.

"Naturally I'm interested in what my children do," said Tessa. "What kind of parent would I be if I weren't? I'm fascinated by their social lives, and I know that they like to confide in me.

"I find it so different from when I was growing up. I envy them, and tell them so.

"And, to show them that we're equals now, I tell them about myself—when I'm happy, when I'm sick, when I'm depressed."

Tessa was happy with the way she treated her children. Were her children happy? From other things she said, her children seemed rather dependent, a conclusion that was strengthened when Tessa told us that her son asked her advice before breaking up with his girlfriend and told her "all the gory details afterward."

Tessa wanted to treat her children as "equals." Is this desirable, or even possible? Although we may be "friends" in the best sense of the word, we are not friends in the literal sense. We are still their parents and they are still our children. Some vestige of authority remains, an authority that can now seem magnified—and uncalled for—when we question them unduly about their personal activities. The authority may be real, assumed, or merely an echo of the past, but it is authority nonetheless. Unspoken is the assumption that when a parent asks a question, a child has to answer. The answer may be true, false, or evasive; it may even take the form of silence. But, whatever form it takes, the whole proceeding raises the issue: Was this question necessary?

Consider some of the consequences that could arise from Tessa's encouraging her son to engage in such "true confession" behavior:

- Her son may keep confiding in her, until one day—to her astonishment—she may find herself listening to something she would rather not hear.
- Her son may eventually blame her for the unhappy outcome of one of his relationships.
- Her son may have difficulty in forming, continuing, or ending a relationship without first consulting his mother.

Some parents unwittingly encourage dependency by delving into their children's lives with a zeal that would be considered way out-of-bounds if they did this to friends. They may, also unwittingly, want to achieve a certain dependent status for *themselves*, by confiding "off limits" subjects—problems in their private lives, problems with their spouses. Often, these questions and confidences are brought forth in a random way, without conscious thought, without any intention to wound, and without thinking about the consequences.

It may be argued that there need not be any "off limits" when a parent speaks to a child—as long as love and respect are present. But intimate confidences can burden an adult child. Most of us will find it helpful to recognize the existence of the gap that lies between the generations. Each generation is part of a specific time frame; each generation grows up with different customs, mores, and beliefs.

One parent told us that to him it is as if parents and children are separated by a "wall."

"My wife and I picture a wall between our children and us," said Warren. "The wall is invisible and sometimes it seems to disappear, but it really is there, and we respect it. We respect our children's opinions and the way they live, even if we would do some things differently. We know that they grew up in a different time."

Warren related a story of when he and his wife, son, and daughter-in-law were driving to the country.

"It was in June, and we had the top down. My wife started singing, and I chimed in. My son and daughter-in-law listened. After a couple of songs, we stopped. Then the kids sang, and we listened.

"After a while, my wife and I began to laugh. 'You know what, kids,' I said. 'We don't know the same songs!' "

As Warren said, the "wall" may seem to disappear at times, but it is there, nonetheless. We can browse around it, take our sturdy ladder called tolerance, curiosity, acceptance, willingness to learn, and climb to the top and look over. We may not be able to enter that territory fully, but we can visit it, and we can acknowledge the existence of both the wall and the life on the other side. We can respect both sides of the wall and show our children to respect them, too. After all, many happily married couples with large age gaps don't always know the same songs either!

Respect: The Golden Key

The key to interacting with children, whether they are babies, adolescents, or adults, is to treat them with respect—respect for them as individuals separate from ourselves, and respect for their jobs, career ambitions, hobbies, and talents. Lack of respect can be shown in a subtle, offhand way.

Charles told us how, without thinking, he had belittled his son's accomplishments.

> "We were talking about a property dispute I was having with my neighbor," said Charles. "My son suggested a certain procedure for me to take. Without thinking, I said, 'Well, I'd better talk to a lawyer first.'
>
> "It was not until the next day that I realized what I had said. After all, my son is a lawyer—and has been a very successful one for several years."

Charles had ignored his son's status unintentionally. The minute he realized what he had done, he called and apologized.

> "Plainly," Charles told his son, "I reverted yesterday to old times—talking to my little boy, forgetting that I was talking to a grown-up professional, and worthy consultant. Thanks for all your advice."

Interwoven with respect is the recognition and acceptance that we no longer have the same authority over our children as we did when they were younger. We may sometimes attempt to prolong their babyhood without realizing it, not necessarily with excessive financial or other help, but by the way we speak to them. No matter how independent, successful, or intelligent they may be, we sometimes react to them as if they were still babies. Are we being controlling without realizing it? We can listen to ourselves. What words do we use, what tone of voice? Do we use such controlling words as "must," "should," "ought," "why didn't you," "why did you"?

In an attempt to hang on to the old authority, some parents speak to their children in unpleasant and inappropriate ways.

We say to a friend who is about to leave for home on a winter night, "The roads are icy." Contrast this with the way some people speak to their children. "The roads are icy, and you know what a maniac you are when you drive in the dark. Stay with us tonight." Love may be hiding somewhere in that sentence, but not respect. We say to a friend, "A macrobiotic diet? Ah. Did you clear it with your doctor?" How many friends would we keep if we said, "A macrobiotic diet? Another idiocy. Last month it was grapefruit, and the month before, rice and black coffee. What's next—sawdust?"

Another way of trying to exert authority is the habit of "mixing in" our children's lives. We can learn to shed the need for control. One woman knew she had conquered her former busybody behavior when a friend said to her, "I hear your son and daughter-in-law bought a fancy sports car. Can they afford it?" In a calm voice, the woman replied, "I don't know. I didn't ask them. But I did tell them it's a pretty car." Silently, the woman congratulated herself. *I've come a long way*, she thought. *A year ago, I would have reacted differently to the kids' new car.*

Advice: Handle With Care

When it comes to giving advice to our children, it is difficult to strike the right note and achieve the right balance. We may think we are being helpful, that we're telling the truth, but is it truth we give, or is it orders, a continuation of the old ploy, "I know better because I'm the parent"?

Giving advice warrants careful thought.

- Discuss the situation first; don't jump right in with rules or platitudes.
- Give advice with caution; be as objective as possible: "Here's my opinion. You may or may not agree."
- Omit the first five words of the classic parent ploy: "Do what you want, but I think . . ."
- Offer advice or an opinion on a specific subject once; twice is one time too many.

- Be calm and unsurprised if the response is negative; do not be hurt if the advice is not taken. If your untaken advice turns out to have been correct, refrain from saying, "I told you so."

If you feel that your child is uncomfortable listening to advice, you may wish to suggest that he or she consult a respected mentor—a friend or family member. If you see that the advice is obviously unwanted, weigh the importance of the issue before giving it:

- Must the advice be given? Is it worth the risk?
- Must you always be right and always in control? If so, the relationship may be jeopardized.
- Are health or other vital issues involved? If so, speak calmly and quietly. You may suggest books or professional care, if appropriate.

Advice is a two-way street. You can ask for it, as well as give it. Asking adult children for their opinions creates a bridge of trust between the generations. You can ask for personal advice—on such subjects as moving, vacations, friends, retiring. You can ask for other kinds of advice, depending on children's occupations, interests, hobbies.

Charles's property dispute required a long and complicated unraveling, but the counsel he received from his son helped Charles to find the right advocate—a specialist in real estate law. Eventually, there was a satisfactory solution and, through it all, Charles enjoyed the support of his son, which gave him the extra dividends of comfort and pride.

Parental Expectations: Realistic or Unreasonable?

Yesterday's dreams—are they today's realities? It can be a bitter disappointment when our dreams for our children do not come to pass. Many of us judge our children by our own standards, even going so far as to measure ourselves by their successes or failures. If they fail, in society's eyes or our own, we feel that we have failed. The child may be a college professor, but we wanted a concert pianist; we got the pianist, but we wanted a partner in our own business—or a lawyer, or a psychologist. What if the child has what we consider a thankless job, or a low-paying job? What if our disappointments go deeper than choice of occupation, if they are entangled with our children's lifestyles, if we find those lifestyles unpalatable or embarrassing? Will we be able to fulfill one of the basic responsibilities of parenthood, that of loving and accepting our children as they are—and as they are not?

Adult children sometimes use their parents as a yardstick. Parents who are ultra-successful or famous can be a hard act to follow. On the other hand, what if the children are glorious successes? Will we measure our own lives by theirs, viewing their successes as either increasing our self-esteem or making us feel inadequate and no longer needed?

We give our children unspoken messages. They know when they have let us down. What results from this knowledge? Take your pick: sorrow, frustration, anger, alienation.

Our disappointments may stem not from the paths our children take, but from our failure to acknowledge to ourselves that they are separate, mature beings. Rooted here may be the grieving for a past that has disappeared and a future that is rapidly shrinking. We may feel that old age is fast upon us, and we are scared.

What do we fear? High on the list—higher, perhaps, than the loss of our physical powers—is the loss of parental power. We had it for so many years, and now it is gone, or going. Some of us hang on by using our last remnants of authority to try to recapture what we once had. Some of us demand detailed reports from our children so that we can evaluate and criticize their behavior, and perhaps pretend to ourselves, consciously or unconsciously, that they are still little:

- "Where were you this weekend?"
- "What time did you get home last night?"
- "Why aren't you wearing your heavy coat?"

Sometimes, we compare our own youth with today's lifestyles.

> "Ah," says the mother, "if only *I* had had a chance at a career and didn't have to take a practical job just for the salary."

> "Ah," says the father, "if only *I* had been able to wander around the country in search of my identity."

Such words are more than wistful longings; they are full of envy and criticism, and both come through loud and clear. We must deal with these feelings by ourselves, without allowing them to damage our relationship with our children.

What is the answer? Do we pussyfoot around our children, afraid to open our mouths; do we "yes" them all the time? The answer lies in treating them with respect, kindness, and humor, and in picturing them as independent adults. Visualizing them this way will hasten the reality.

From time to time, review in your mind some of the elementary and helpful ways you can start to let go:

- Trust your children, and let them know it.
- Recognize that your children are separating, and discuss it with them.
- Show confidence in their ability to run their own lives.
- Encourage them to set and pursue their own goals.
- Offer emotional support.
- Acknowledge and praise their accomplishments.
- Be loving if they stumble, and share with them stories of when *you* stumbled.

We are bound to regress now and then into old patterns. Who would not, after all those years of active parenting?

A mother and daughter were on their way out the door when visitors arrived to see another member of the family. The mother explained the reason for their hasty departure. "*We* are going shopping," she said. "*We* are going out to buy *us* a raincoat."

As soon as the words left her mouth, she realized how patronizing she sounded.

But the mother was lucky. Or wise. She had all these years created a climate of trust and camaraderie within her family that enabled her daughter, when they were alone in the car, to say, "Honestly, Ma, for a moment you made me feel like a helpless little girl, unable to go shopping without her 'mommy.' "

"Sweetie, I know it," said the mother. "I realized right away how silly I sounded. Be gentle with me, hon; it's hard to teach an old dog new tricks."

Mother and daughter had a hearty laugh.

Good lesson. Happy ending. Both mother and daughter were aware of what had happened, acknowledged the situation, and laughed about it.

Life repeatedly presents opportunities to bring us ever closer to letting go. We still may make some mistakes. We would really be overconfident if we perceived ourselves as infallible, or even close to it. As a matter of fact, it can be comforting to acknowledge that we are not perfect, that we can make mistakes and go on—that things will be all right.

The ultimate test is for us to be able to speak to and listen to our children in a respectful and nonjudgmental way.

Letting go gives us and our adult children the freedom to slough off old images and build new ones, and to rethink and restructure our lives.

From time to time, we can ask ourselves if we have succeeded in achieving an equal, independent relationship with our children. Do we have the results we want? If we have not yet succeeded fully, that is not a cause for despair. The process takes time. Just remember: If we let our children go lovingly and willingly, they will not go far.

Reflections

1. Go back in time, to when you were roughly the age your children are now.

   • Did the relationship between you and your parents change after you reached the magic age of twenty-one?
   • Did your parents speak differently to you, act differently? Did they treat you with respect, as befitting your new adult status?

2. Think back to how you would like to have been treated. Is there much of a gap?

3. Now make the big leap: How have you been treating your own children? First, think of your past role as parent of a *young* child. Then, think of your present role as parent of a *grown* child.

   • How do the two roles differ?
   • How does *your* behavior differ?
   • Are there changes you would like to make?
   • How can you help yourself make these changes?

4. Think about how you treat the grown children of your friends or other young people of the same age.

   • Do you accord more respect to them than you do to your own child?
   • Are there changes you would like to make?

Quick Steps to Letting Go

Awareness

- Don't get stuck in the old patterns of parenting.
- Watch for clues that you and your children are beginning to separate:
    Are you spending less time together?
    Do you need fewer "daily weather reports"?
    Are you happy to be together, happy to be apart?

Acceptance

- Accept the fact that your children have one foot out the door—perhaps you should buy a smaller refrigerator!

Acknowledgment

- Recognize that your children have lives apart from yours.
- Applaud your children's successes even if they don't match your dreams.
- Consult your children when you want advice; you might learn something.

Action

- Listen more, tell less.
- Take a deep breath; reorganize your priorities; allow your parental reins to slip away.
- Focus on the next chapter of your life.
- Enjoy your newfound freedom!

Chapter 2

Communication:
The Open Door

Good communication nourishes a relationship; poor communication starves it.

What are the benefits of good communication?

- News or information
- Expressions of caring
- Advice—seeking or giving
- Sharing ideas, opinions, and concerns

Communication between parent and child should alter as the child grows into adulthood and the generation gap diminishes. As a young person matures and develops greater understanding, parent and child are more able to speak to each other as adult to adult. If we are not aware of this development, misunderstanding or resentment is likely to develop. What a joy it is to be able to share ideas and news with your adult children. Your relationship can grow more intimate as you exchange concerns and brainstorm problems with one another.

What positive results can be gained from good communication between you and your adult children?

- Comfort and ease with one another
- Closeness and warmth
- Loyalty and trust

In short, communication is the dynamic that can enhance a relationship and move it forward.

If your communication is "missing the mark," it is like having a defective spark plug in your car, which causes the engine to sputter and gives you a bumpy ride.

Think now of the communication between you and your adult child. Is it healthy and strong, or forced and stale? Does it take into consideration your child's adult status? Is it up-to-date, or are you stuck in a time-warp, mistakenly dealing with your child as if he were a youngster or an adolescent? What kind of communication would you like: more, less, or a different kind? Does what you have now contain the elements needed to create a relationship of respect and trust?

Respect and Trust

Respect can be thought of as a "Golden Key" that opens the door to any good relationship. Without it, the door remains shut, and the relationship suffocates.

Ruth, the mother of a married daughter, said that her child rarely came to see her.

> "I hardly saw her between January and June," Ruth told us.
> "As for telephone calls, I have to leave four or five messages on her answering machine before she'll call me back."

When asked why she thought this was so—did her daughter live far away, did she have young children, did she have a busy work schedule, had there been a disagreement between mother and daughter—Ruth replied that her daughter lived half an hour away, and had no children and lots of free time.

"So, why does she treat me this way?" Ruth asked. "What did I do?"

What did Ruth do? She saw herself as a loving, interested mother. Upon further discussion, however, it turned out that she was a little *too* interested. Ruth admitted her tendency to ask too many questions and give too much advice, whether it was requested or not.

"My daughter told me that because of what I said at the cousins' meeting, I'd never be able to worm anything out of her again. I told her that everybody sympathized with her, so why was she getting so excited?"

Ruth then divulged what had happened. At a family gathering, with her daughter and son-in-law present, Ruth announced to the entire assemblage that her daughter had been trying for several months to become pregnant.

Ruth's daughter and son-in-law were shocked and embarrassed at Ruth's disclosure. They felt their privacy had been violated. It was not their intention to discuss their private matters with such a large family group. They felt that it was their business and their business alone to decide where and when such matters should be discussed.

It took Ruth a long time to acknowledge that she had not only been treating her daughter like a baby, but as someone unworthy of respect.

"I guess," said Ruth, "that's what my daughter meant when she said she wanted to live her own life. I guess maybe I wanted to live it for her a little bit."

A parent who behaves in this way is the loser in the relationship, losing the adult child's respect and trust. She probably will not be told anything again in confidence.

Ruth's complaint that she rarely saw her daughter showed that she either ignored or was unaware of the poor quality of the little time they did have together. When she finally came to realize how she had betrayed her daughter's confidence, Ruth went about trying to mend the relationship. She left messages on her daughter's answering machine, saying things like, "I was wrong." "I'm sorry." "Can't we get together?"

It took a while before the daughter would consent to see her mother, but eventually she did. They began to meet for lunch and for an occasional movie. It took much longer before they discussed family matters, and then only in a limited way. As far as a closer, more intimate relationship was concerned, it was uncertain if that would ever come to pass.

A good relationship needs nurturing. Actively cultivate ways to enhance respect and trust.

- Acknowledge that your children are mature individuals.
- Respect your children's right to privacy; respect their confidences.

At an informal gathering of old friends, a father was describing his relationship with his son. "My son tells me everything." He spoke smugly and with absolute confidence. The man truly believed that his son did and should reveal to him all the important details of his life.

But did the son tell his father *everything*? Or was the father assuming a level of intimacy that did not exist? Should a child confide all the details of his life to his parent? What level of intimacy is appropriate between parent and child? A parent who believes that the child confides everything may also assume that he, as parent, deserves a role in the young person's decision making.

We might be talking about a single person making important decisions about career choice, lifestyle, or love life. We might be talking about a young married person dealing with marriage, children, home, career, or any other important facets of life.

Parents are right to be interested and, we hope, continuously supportive. However, we want to guard against intruding upon the young adult's independence, or interfering with what are the young person's own decisions to make.

As the good parents we hope to remain always, we should try to keep some guidelines in mind:

- Avoid asking probing questions such as:
  "How much did you pay for that couch?"
  "When are you going to start a family?"
  Such questions are intrusive, judgmental, and—*bad manners*!
- Find the degree of intimacy that is right for you and right for them.
- Differentiate between sharing and excessive burdening on either side.
- Discourage very intimate disclosure.
  "My children tell me everything."
  Do they really? And do you really want to know?
- Review your own conduct to see if you have invited too much disclosure.

Parents should also guard against revealing to their children intimate stories of their own.

Martin told us how what he meant as a humorous story embarrassed his family.

"The children were telling us about their friends, about their careers, and about who was living with whom. I began to think that maybe they were telling some of these stories for shock effect. Without thinking, I revealed a secret that they had never heard before.

" 'You kids think you're so modern,' I blurted out.

'Mother and I lived together—secretly, of course—for six months before we were married.'

"The minute I said this, I was sorry I let the cat out of the bag. My son gave a nervous laugh, my daughter cried out, 'Ma!' and my wife turned red and immediately left the room."

Martin had merely wanted to enter into the spirit of his children's conversation. He wanted his children to regard him as a modern man who was with it, but his story shocked the whole family. Martin overstepped the line when he shared an intimacy that his children would have preferred not to know.

Attitude: The Messages We Send

Are you dissatisfied with the responses you receive from your adult children? Could it be your attitude that evokes a negative reply, or no reply at all?

One parent told us that he knew when he was on "shaky ground" with his son by the way the young man uttered a few "uh-huhs" and then abruptly changed the subject.

"All I did," said Bert, "was tell Ron to start looking for a job with a bigger salary. I meant it for his own good. He's always selling himself short. Sometimes I just don't know what's bothering the kid."

One of the main irritations that Ron experienced was that his father thought of him as a "kid." Bert had not yet made the leap to recognizing that his son had grown into adulthood.

Many parents do not take responsibility if the communication between them and their adult children is less than satisfactory.

One parent described his weekly telephone conversation with his adult son.

"I was sitting here waiting for your call," Leonard told his son. "I was afraid to leave the apartment, in case I'd miss you. Just hearing your voice, just knowing that you'll call soon, makes the sun shine all day for me."

Did Leonard think he was complimenting or soothing his son? Or was he using him for his own ends? It is easy to picture the adult child conjuring up a vision of his lonely, anxious father sitting and waiting for the telephone to ring. The *sun* may be shining with rays of warmth and happiness for the parent, but surely the *rain* is pouring torrents of guilt onto the child.

Leonard claimed that he has "great success" with the way he speaks to his child. Maybe he does, but for how long, and with what results? What is the value of such "success"? At best, it seems nothing more than a forced ritual founded on guilt; at worst, it can be summed up in one word: manipulation. It is fine to tell your child that the sun shines when you hear his voice, as long as those words are not a code for, "Pity me; I'm all alone; I have nothing to do but wait for you to call me." How much better it would be for the parent to just *sound* as if the sun were shining when the child calls, to sound cheerful and happy to hear the child's voice, and to have interesting items and subjects to contribute to the conversation.

You may think that you're delivering a certain message to your child, but your child may hear something entirely different.

Parent *asks*: "Are you still living in that large apartment?"
Child *hears*: "You don't know how to spend money."

Parent *asks*: "Is that the jacket you wear to work?"
Child *hears*: "You've never known how to dress properly."

Parent *asks*: "Another party? Aren't you tired?"
Child *hears*: "You're always going out; I'm always alone."

Parent *asks*: "Did you hear that Betty Ann is engaged?"
Child *hears*: "When are you going to get married?"

Listen to yourself. Your child may be picking up vibes from your communication that contradict your words. Your tone of voice or your hand gestures may not match your spoken words. On the other hand, your child may be sensitive to issues that caused upsets in the growing-up years.

Develop a sensitivity and awareness. Attempt to anticipate your child's response to your question. You may want to rephrase your communication, or decide to drop the issue altogether. If you make a "mistake," clear it up right then and there.

If you feel misunderstood by your adult child, check yourself:

- Is what you say what you mean to say?
- Does your tone of voice support what you wish to convey?
- Does your child understand you in the way you wish to be understood?

Recognize Your Emotions and Express Them

Events in our lives awaken emotions, both positive and negative. Our expressions of joy and happiness are usually well received by others. We may not be able to handle our feelings of anger and frustration as easily. Negative feelings of anger toward our children may evoke guilt within ourselves. We may also fear rejection by our adult children once we have expressed our upset. As a result, it is not uncommon for a parent to decide to "keep quiet and swallow it." Unfortunately, such a stance can end in aborted communication. The child correctly recognizes the anger by the parent's silence, body language, grimaces, and general withdrawal. The net result is that parent and child come to an impasse. Stop and reflect. How do you wish to be with your adult children? Loving? Friendly? Joyful? What must you do to achieve that?

Perhaps in reviewing a situation that made you angry in the

past, you may decide that the issue was not really that important and you're sorry you didn't "let go." Or, you decide that you had to "clear" with your child in order to go forward with your relationship.

- Avoid yelling, scolding, accusing, blaming. Such outbursts will not bring you the results you want.
- Express your feelings by sharing your perception of what upset you.
- Talk about the circumstance rather than the individuals involved.

During a group counseling session, one father expressed his rage at his son. The son had requested a gift of money from his father to be used as start-up capital for a small business. The father, eager to see his son successful, readily dug into his pocket. The son, an inveterate gambler, lost the money at the gaming tables the next night.

Understandably, the father felt used and abused. He was counseled to express just that to his son rather than to rant and rave.

The father confronted the son with a direct statement. "I feel used and abused. If you enroll in Gamblers' Anonymous, you and I have a chance."

The son agreed to follow his father's recommendation, and he took a job in order to pay his debts. Although the father had decided not to give his son monetary gifts anymore, he did express support and acknowledgment regarding the positive steps his son was taking toward recovery. This process resulted in honest and respectful communication between father and son.

As a result of the counseling, the father understood that there was a risk in telling his son, "I feel used and abused." The son may very well have turned away from his father. Nevertheless, the father chose to express himself honestly. He was hoping for a "win-win" result: a reconciliation with his son.

Rechannel Your Anger To Have It Become a Positive Energy

- Use your feelings of anger positively to move toward desired results.
- Anticipate your child's response.
- Express yourself in a manner that will bring you closer to your adult child.
- Start with an "I" statement. Tell how you feel.
- Express anger toward the deed or circumstance, not the individual.
- Express your feelings honestly and as calmly as you can.
- Aim for a "win-win" situation—satisfaction for all concerned.

Listen

Listening is as much an art as speaking is. Good listening requires your undivided attention. Listening includes tuning in to the underlying agenda of the person delivering the message.

A daughter complained to her mother: "Pat plays golf every weekend with his clients. He's never home. He hasn't mowed the lawn in weeks." The underlying message is, "I'm lonely. I would like to spend some fun time with him."

In this situation, just listening and permitting the daughter to tell her story might be enough. If she asks for a solution to her problem, the mother will then be able to address the real issue—being left alone—rather than how to get the lawn mowed.

Listen to your child intently. Keep your mind clear to receive your child's message. If you don't let your own thoughts and judgments interfere, you will understand more fully what is being told to you. Your total attention will diminish your need to interrupt with your own stories and opinions. Your child will appreciate the respect exhibited by your being a good listener.

Intelligent listening occasionally requires that the listener interrupt in order to clarify what is being told. A daughter reported to her father, "Dave and I decided that we would get married Saturday." The father thought she meant that she planned to be married the following Saturday. Thinking that his daughter might be pregnant, he was startled and asked anxiously, "Is there any reason that you must rush into marriage?" The daughter, laughing, answered, "Oh, Dad, I meant to say that *last* Saturday we made a commitment and will probably set a date for this coming spring."

It was a good thing that the father asked for immediate clarification of his daughter's ambiguous announcement.

Learn to listen.

- Give your undivided attention.
- Tune in to the underlying message.
- Wait to be asked before suggesting solutions.
- Don't joke or make light of your children's concerns.
- Respond with respect; avoid sarcasm.

Tell the Truth

Do your conversations with your adult children accurately represent your feelings?

Do you say "yes" to a request made by your child when your facial expression says "no"?

Does your child have to guess what you really would like to say?

At times it takes courage to tell the truth. You may be fearful of rejection by your children. You may be concerned about damaging your relationship with them. You may feel guilty about not being the "good parent."

The day that Natalie had dreaded for years finally arrived. Her adopted daughter announced that she had started to search for her birth mother.

Natalie felt threatened. She questioned whether she had

truly been a good mother. Why else would her daughter be looking for another mother?

She feared that she would be rejected and lose her daughter's love. She was anxious about being compared to the other woman. How would she fare? She also asked herself what might happen to her family unit. She was frightened.

Natalie went to the library to seek current information regarding adopted children. She then visited the agency from which she had adopted her daughter and asked for advice and support. The counselor at the agency reassured Natalie that what her daughter was doing was not unusual. She encouraged Natalie to share with her daughter the truth about how she felt.

Natalie followed the counselor's advice and shared her feelings with her daughter. As a result, mother and daughter grew closer than they had ever been.

The daughter came away from the discussion understanding what worried her mother. Natalie was able to calm her own fears by repeating to herself her daughter's words, "Mom, I love you. You will always be my mother."

Telling the truth about your feelings protects the integrity of your relationship.

- Consider first what you really want to say.
- Tell the truth in the best possible way in order to avoid hurting your child.
- Start with an "I" statement ("I feel hurt") rather than casting blame ("You hurt me").
- Rehearse your conversation. Talk about the circumstance: "I felt left out when I was not introduced to your friend," rather than, "You never introduce me when you meet a friend by chance. Are you ashamed of me?"
- Tell only as much truth as you believe will move your relationship forward. For example, "I would like to have lunch

with you alone one day." It is not necessary to add, "Your wife is a dodo, and always puts her two cents into our conversation."

- Tell the truth regarding a serious health problem you may have. Keeping such information to yourself may lead your children to believe you don't trust them to give you the support you need. On the other hand, don't burden them by reporting every little hangnail.

Consider whether what is on your mind is really important to share. Is it necessary to express your distaste for some new furnishings purchased by your adult children? Will telling them that you don't like their lamps or their couch make them feel good about themselves—or you? They may become angry—understandably so. Would you be so blunt with a friend?

When asked for an opinion, tell the truth in a way that will nurture your relationship with your child, rather than wound it.

Gwen's daughter asked for her opinion of a dress purchased in a final sale. The mother did not care for the garment, but replied, "I think you have some clothes in your wardrobe that are more flattering."

Gwen avoided saying, "You don't know how to shop for yourself. Next time I'll go with you."

Tell the truth to the right person. If your son-in-law returns the car with an empty tank, don't complain to your daughter. Have courage. Say to your son-in-law, "Please fill up the gas tank before you return my car." Your statement need not be delivered angrily. Simply assert your wishes.

The reward for being appropriately truthful with your child is a relationship built on trust and integrity.

Reflections

1. If you would like to improve the conversations you have with your children, play back in your mind some recent talks. Answer these questions:
   - Do you bark out orders? Do you tell your children what to do, where to go, and how to spend their time and their money?
   - Do you ask questions of an intimate nature?
   - Do you routinely give unsolicited advice?
   - Do you give solicited advice in a commanding way, as if to imply that yours is the only proper course of action?

2. Think of several friendships you value highly. What do you talk about with these good friends? Do you talk about serious things? Do you also tell jokes, describe your tennis game, discuss the latest movie? The same good practices that serve you in making and keeping your friends will help you enrich the communication with your adult children.

Exercises

1. Set your child's picture next to a mirror and pretend you are talking to your child. See yourself as your child sees you. Watch your face. Listen to your voice.
   - What do you see; what do you hear: criticism? disapproval? demands? instructions? advice? questions? prying questions?
   - Are these the things you wish to convey? Do your voice and your words convey your real feelings?
   - Is love evident? Is there real exchange in the conversation? Any witty repartee? Any subject other than parent-child matters—politics, art, literature, sports, people?

2. Look in the mirror and imagine a conversation that will include the same subjects you spoke about with your child—but this time talk to a friend.

3. Look in the mirror and have a frank conversation with your child about your feelings or about any part of your relationship.

4. Visualize your children speaking to you.
   - Do they soft-pedal, play down, evade answers? "Oh, I didn't do much on the weekend."
   - Listen to your part of the conversation: "Don't tell me you went out with *him* again!" (After a while, she *won't* tell you.)

5. Words can help or hurt. Do you use the traditional parental words: should ... must ... ought ... why did you? ... why didn't you? ... why don't you? ... why won't you?
   - Prepare some sentences using these words.
   - Now, rephrase these sentences *without* these words.
   - How does the second group of sentences differ from the first?

6. If you are uncomfortable speaking to your child about a particular issue, write a letter. In telling the "truth" on paper:
   - You are not distracted by the other person's defensiveness.
   - You have an opportunity to edit your message.
   - You can eliminate superfluous material, blame, or apology.
   - You may become clearer through the process of writing as to the results you want.
   - You have the opportunity to take your time and rephrase your statement in order to avoid being hurtful.
   - You have the choice after composing the letter and reading it to send it or tear it up.

Will sending the letter get you the results you want? Just writing it may serve your needs.

7. Body language, facial expressions, hand gestures all reveal what a person means to communicate. Next time you're in a restaurant, pay attention to people around you. Observe them in an ongoing conversation. Without hearing their words, can you guess the nature of their discussion?

- What emotions can you identify?
- What do you see that you wish to avoid in your own conversations: Inattention? Disapproval? Boredom?

Chapter 3

Money: The Invisible Hook

"Money can't buy love," says the comic, "but it sure puts you in an excellent bargaining position."

As part of a comedy routine, that joke is amusing; it ceases to be funny when applied to family relationships. In matters concerning one's children, using money to bargain or control is sure to bring negative results. The newspapers are full of stories about families who wrangle over money and then become estranged, sometimes for life. This kind of wrangling and aim for control is also used by people whose stories do not make the headlines. Sometimes this is done deliberately, sometimes unintentionally.

"I'll give you a hundred dollars—or a thousand—*if* . . ."

"Marry that guy, and I'll cut you off without a cent."

"That junk heap? It'll fall apart before you get it home. I'll get you a better car than that."

Bribes, threats, crutches. All of these stand in the way of healthy relationships between parents and adult children.

Money can be used as a positive force, buying necessities,

comfort, and pleasure. If, however, we allow it to be the main focus of our lives, or if we let it direct all our actions, then it becomes a hook, sharp and puncturing, controlling us in the same way we may try to control others. We can hide the hook by covering it with offerings that camouflage our true intent. We can even fool ourselves into believing that we "only meant it for the best."

Money becomes a teaching tool early in the parenting process. Without realizing it, we impart our own attitudes to our children.

"You spent two weeks' allowance on baseball cards? How could you do such a thing?"

"You spent everything on candy? Here's another two dollars. Feel better now?"

"Survival camp? Do you want to break your neck? How would you like a new bicycle instead—that ten-speed job you wanted? Does that make you feel better about spending a summer at home?"

In the first example, both the child's purchase and judgment are belittled; in the second, the child is told that the parent will always be there to bail him or her out; in the third, the child is bribed with an expensive gift.

When our children were very young, we relinquished a measure of control by teaching them to walk without holding on. As the years progressed, we encouraged them to develop various aspects of independence. Now we can encourage them to develop financial independence, thus giving them the freedom, the joy, and the power of financial responsibility.

As in every area of family relationships, there is no one right way to use money, but there are comfortable ways for each of us. We have to find those ways. Coming into play, as they do with every aspect of our interaction with our children, are the components we spoke of earlier: communication, truth, respect, and attitude. These components are intertwined and inseparable. How we treat our children and how we speak to them, about money or anything else, form the backbone of our relationship with them.

Gift Giving

As the proverb says, " 'Tis better to give than to receive." But there can be a dark side to gift giving. Sometimes, the parent attaches a message to the gift. The message may be obvious or not, conscious or not. The message may be one of love, guilt, lack of confidence in the child, or an attempt to keep the child psychologically tied. When you give a gift purely out of love, the love comes through and the message is received; when you give a gift out of guilt or some other motive, that message is also received.

How happy parents feel when they give their children gifts. The parent says:

- "Lunch is on me today."
- "I bought this for myself and I thought you would enjoy one, too."
- "Come with us on the trip. We got you tickets."

Depending on the nature of the relationship, the child may hear:

- "I love you and want you to have something nice." [Love]
- "I want to make amends for not being around more when you were little." [Guilt]
- "I want something from you." [Bribe]
- "I'm sorry I criticized you last week." [Apology]
- "I bought this for you because I know you'll never be able to buy it for yourself." [Put-down]
- "I give you presents so you won't leave me." [Control]
- "I don't want to let go; I can't let go." [More control]

Turn Negative Reactions Into Positive Ones

- Be aware of *what* you offer your children.
- Practice listening to yourself—the words you use, the gestures, the tone of voice.
- Analyze your child's reaction to the gift.
    Do you think the reaction was justified?
    How could you have brought about a different reaction, either by a different presentation or a different gift?
- Talk *with*—not *to*—your child about the gift.

Even the size of a gift can tell a story. Too small a gift may express disapproval; too large a gift, the desire to prolong the child's dependency. Keep in mind the relative qualities of the words *small* and *large*. Each family has its own definitions.

What if you give a gift, but are disappointed by the child's response?

"I gave my daughter an antique chair," said Edna. "It was her grandmother's—solid mahogany, a real beauty. I expected a big hug and a kiss. And what happened? Cathy put it in the attic. She said she was afraid to keep it in the living room. Her kids are still too young."

What are you to do? You love your child and want to demonstrate that love.

Ask Yourself Some Questions

- Is the gift appropriate?
- Is it one that the child will want?
- Does it have a hidden purpose?

Gifts such as a book or a restaurant lunch can be offered in a spontaneous way unless they're given too often and come to be expected or even resented. Gifts such as a vacation or a piece of furniture need more thought beforehand. Is a hook lurking somewhere? Does the child wish to go on this particular trip— and with the parents? Will the child, or perhaps the child's spouse, feel too beholden to the parents?

Edna was already on the road to the truth when she admitted she was looking for "a big hug and a kiss." Fine. By itself, that's a nice motive. By traveling down the road a bit, she was able to admit, "It would have been wiser if I had asked Cathy what she needed rather than giving her the chair before she could enjoy it. When I did ask her what she would like from among her grandmother's treasures, she asked for the heirloom cradle."

Edna had more than truth going for her. Her attitude was positive. She wasn't overly hurt or insulted; she was willing to communicate with Cathy by asking what Cathy would like—and she treated Cathy with respect. Edna got an added bonus. Letting Cathy choose her gift not only satisfied Edna's wish to give her daughter an heirloom, but told Edna that her daughter was receiving something she wanted and could use.

In the best sense, gifts are symbols of a parent's love. But giving something without thinking of the child may interfere with this symbolism. The best gift is one the child will truly enjoy and that is appropriate at the time. A gift may be inappropriate if it is given at the wrong time; it may also be the wrong gift— a gift with a hook at the end of it.

> Jim loved every sport ever invented. His son Kenneth had never shown an aptitude for sports or the desire to learn.
>
> For his son's birthday, Jim bought him a squash racket. Kenneth looked at the gift, laughed, and said, "Won't you ever give up trying to make me over in your image?"

What is critical here is not only the son's words, but also the way he said them. He laughed. Was this a real laugh, good-natured and lighthearted, or was it sardonic? Was the laugh accompanied by clenched fists and tight lips, showing that— rightly or wrongly—Kenneth felt the gift was meant to point out his inadequacies as a sportsman and perhaps as a son?

What if your adult child asks for a gift that you feel is either unsuitable or too expensive? Saying yes makes you feel resentful; saying no makes you feel guilty. How do you say no to a request and still remain a good parent?

Mark wanted a compact disc player for his birthday, a gift that would cost considerably more than his parents had wished to spend. At first, they decided against buying it, but this made them feel mean and stingy.

What did they do? They bought it.

How did they feel? They resented the amount of money; they felt almost victimized. Mark's father grumbled to his wife: "If Mark is supposed to be an adult now, why do we have to spend so much money on his birthday?"

What were the results? Mark's birthday was a disaster. The parents hardly said a word when they presented the gift. Months later, they still didn't mention it. Mark, perhaps feeling guilty about the whole thing, didn't mention it either, nor did he play any music when his parents visited him in his apartment.

What could the parents have done to avoid such unpleasantness? They could have told him the truth, that this particular item cost more than they planned to spend. They then could have given him their intended amount of money, so that he could either pool it with his, or start saving until he had enough to buy the item.

Be careful that under the guise of, "It's too much money; I can't afford it," you are not masking the truth—that the child's choice displeases you. Such behavior can be an attempt to control the child through money.

Sometimes a gift is not perceived as a gift.

When Bob and Helen married, Bob's parents offered to pay for furnishing their apartment. To this offer, a little string was attached—the unspoken understanding that the young people were expected to choose a place close to the parents' house.

Was this a gift or a means of maintaining control? The parents viewed their offer as a generous one, but it would have had more validity without a condition tied to it.

Bob and Helen felt they were being controlled and that, if they accepted, both their relationship with each other and their relationship with Bob's parents would be damaged. The young couple turned down the offer by saying they had already signed a lease for the apartment they wanted.

The parents were dumbfounded. The apartment the couple chose—on the other side of the city—was almost identical to the one near the parents' house. When the parents talked about it between themselves, they began to remember the days when *they* were newlyweds and set great value on independence.

"Maybe we were too pushy," said Bob's mother. "I suppose they want their privacy. Should we buy them the furniture anyway?"

"Hm," said Bob's father, "let's decide how much money we'll give them, and then they can buy what they like."

A Guide to Gift Giving

- When you give money, be clear in your own mind if it is for a specific purpose or is to be used at the child's discretion.
- Is a message attached to your gift? Is a hook attached? Do you want something in return for the gift?
- Give a gift that you feel will please the recipient.

- Enjoy the reward you get from giving a gift: the pleasure it brings both to you and your child.
- Give a gift so that the recipient feels loved and cared for—and not diminished.
- If you're about to give a sizable gift, ask if your child really wants it.
- If your child asks for a gift that you cannot or do not want to give, discuss the matter with your child. If the cost is too steep, say so.

Gift Giving Works Both Ways

How do you react when your child wants to give you a gift? Not a sweater for your birthday, or a book for Mother's Day or Father's Day, but a weekend at a resort or a cruise, or some other indulgence you could not afford yourself.

"Our children," said a father, "knew that we had always dreamed of going to the Costa del Sol in Spain. They surprised us on our anniversary with plane tickets and hotel reservations.

"It took me a while to be comfortable with accepting such a lavish gift. I finally realized that by accepting graciously I was giving our children as much a gift as they were giving us."

Communicating Financial Status

How much specific information about your financial status should you share with your children? The answer is: everything, nothing, or anything in between—the choice is yours.

Whatever you decide, you have already, consciously or not, conveyed much. You don't have to hand over tax returns or bank books to let your children know how you regard money, and how you spend it. They learn these things from childhood observations. The house you live in, the clothing you wear, the vacations you take all reveal part of the picture. By no means, however, do they reveal the whole story. Diamonds around the neck are not a sure sign of money in the bank.

If you decide to fill your children in on your financial resources, it does not mean that you have to have a "true confession session" in which to bare your soul. It is up to you to decide how much to disclose. As one parent said, "We gave our children a very general idea of our assets, without naming exact items or amounts. This way, we feel we maintain our privacy and independence."

Sharing financial information—no matter how minimal—can show children that parents consider them mature, thereby creating trust and mutual respect between the generations. It can promote a close relationship or enhance an already close one. The information may aid the children in making their own financial decisions. In addition, they may have some advice to offer their parents.

Equally as important as sharing details about money is sharing feelings about it—how you regard earning, saving, spending, and giving it. You can also share your plans for your own future. These talks help to explain later actions and reduce the mystique that so often surrounds the subject of money.

> The Johnsons called a family conference shortly before the marriage of their daughter. At the meeting were the daughter's fiancé, their daughter-in-law, and all of their children, the youngest of whom was a senior in high school.
>
> "We want to give you a general look at our financial picture," said the father, "and to establish a feeling of confidence that will bond us all into a unit."
>
> He then proceeded to speak of his and his wife's retirement plans, expected education expenses, assets, and resources.
>
> The meeting was a success. Josh, the youngest, said, "I

feel good that you think of me as an adult." Mike, the fiancé, felt honored to be considered a family member.

Whether or not you decide to share financial information, a list of your assets plus the names of lawyer, accountant, stockbroker, and other professional advisers, as well as the location of deeds, wills, and similar documents, are useful for your own peace of mind, as well as that of your children. Such a list can ease your transition into a stage when you may want or need to share more information.

Money and Long-term Goals

More than money is involved in financing children's higher education or career plans. Parents often envision their children in certain careers. What happens when the dreams of having an attorney or a business tycoon or an opera singer do not materialize? Do you moan, do you coax, do you stare at them stonily and silently? Do you withdraw your love? Do you use the power of money to threaten or bribe?

"Did I slave all my life," asked a father, "so that my son could become an actor? I'm not paying for such nonsense!"

The father argued back and forth with himself before finally deciding that it was important to accept his son's choice of career. He then agreed to pay for acting school.

"My husband and I built this business from scratch," said a mother. "We assumed the kids would come in with us. Now one wants to buy a farm and the other wants to be a social worker—which means another two years in school.

"We want the kids to be happy, but there's no getting away from it—we're disappointed."

Disappointment is often the result if we try to force our children into molds of our own making. The son who did not want the squash racket accused his father of trying to "make me over in your image." We have to ask ourselves if this is what we are doing—and it's a common practice. Many of us measure success by our personal standards instead of considering our children's ambitions and desires. If we associate our own desires with money, and use money as a means of satisfying those desires, conflict is bound to ensue.

Communication is at the core of any relationship. As you talk with your children about education and careers, you will learn about their plans for the future, and at the same time express your own hopes, fears, and recommendations.

Amy was the "family artist." Upon graduating from college, she talked about setting up a studio. Would her parents stake her to a year's rent?

The parents were willing, but pointed out to their daughter the value of commercial art training as an added bit of security. They remembered their own early career struggles and shared these stories with Amy.

Together they talked it over and together they came up with the plan that Amy would take a year's training in whatever branch of commercial art pleased her. After the training, if Amy still wished, the parents would help pay for a studio.

Both Amy and her parents felt confident that the extra training would pave the way for Amy's studio career.

It is important that parents be willing to accept their children's own visions for their future.

Think About Your Aspirations for Your Adult Child

• If your aspirations are very different from your child's, try to consider if they are practical and logical for him or her.

What is the worst thing that could happen if your child pursues his own desires? (Would your child fall off the earth? Or would you be embarrassed to explain to friends the career your child has chosen?)

- If your child wants a career you do not like, examine your reasons. Are you trying to project your own past ambitions or longings onto your child?
- Talk with your child about his goals. Give your opinions in a nonjudgmental way. Give any recommendations the same way.

Loans

Money is generally equated with power. When you lend money to your child, be careful not to use the money as a hook to exercise this power, or to slow down your child's independence.

When a loan is made through a bank, both parties know where they stand. Amounts are set, as are dates for repayment. Loans made on a personal basis, especially those to children, require advance thought and planning. Here, business is combined with emotions, a volatile mix.

A bank asks the would-be borrower the purpose of the loan. A commercial enterprise? A house? A car? A parent also wants to know why the money is requested. What if you feel that the money is wanted for a frivolous reason? If you make the loan anyway, will you feel resentful, or that you have been "taken"? How will you feel if the money is not repaid? If you refuse to make the loan, will you jeopardize the relationship?

Previous experience can help with decision making.

When Trudy entered college, her parents gave her a credit card. Trudy used it for school supplies and a small luxury now and then. Every month, she submitted the receipts to her parents. They were pleased with the way she handled everything, but not surprised. Trudy had always been prudent with money.

When Trudy wanted to start a business, her parents did not hesitate to lend her money. The money was lent on an informal basis because her parents knew that Trudy kept scrupulous records and would start a repayment plan as soon as possible.

Richard's parents told a different story.

They were nervous when Richard wanted to borrow money to buy into a partnership. Although proud of his sales skills, they knew his track record with money. Richard had never been able to stay on his allowance, and even as an adult never knew where his money went.

The parents considered refusing the request, but soon rejected the idea. They told Richard that the loan would be made in a businesslike way, with everything spelled out on paper—the full amount of the loan, and the timing and structuring of the payments.

Richard was embarrassed. "You don't trust me, do you?"

The father held his ground. "On the contrary, Richard, we're sure you'll succeed in this venture, and we know you'll repay the money. By setting up this schedule, we feel we're treating you like the professional you are. Well, what do you say to that?"

Richard grinned. "You won't be sorry."

By spelling out the details in a businesslike and loving way, the parents were able to protect their interests while still showing a willingness to help.

One couple said that they had agreed to lend their child twenty thousand dollars toward the down payment of a house. They had responded to the request with eagerness, but, afterward, when the two of them talked it over, they realized that they would be surrendering a considerable amount of interest. They decided to discuss this with their child in order to come up with a satisfactory arrangement, and they included interest in the repayment.

As near as possible, parents' needs, as well as the children's, must be met. A schedule can be drawn to satisfy everyone.

What happens if parents invest in a child's business and the business fails? Such a misfortune affects all the participants. The child suffers loss of self-esteem, as well as discomfort over the parents' loss. The parents are disappointed by their judgment and their child's judgment. On top of everything, the parents suffer because their child is hurt.

Parents and child have to act quickly to prevent the misfortune from escalating into tragedy. Blighted hopes, loss of self-respect, sorrow over the financial loss, sorrow for the child, sorrow for the parents—these feelings, if unexpressed, can damage the parent-child relationship. By talking things over, the family members will reinforce their closeness and start to find ways to overcome their financial problems.

When Parents Differ

Rose was troubled over the frequent requests for money made by her son Maury to his father.

"If Jed keeps giving him money, Maury will never be able to stand on his own two feet. I want my son to be an independent adult. The fact that Jed and I disagree about giving money to Maury is creating tremendous tension between us."

Rose decided to tell Jed about her fears for their son's future, and that she felt that giving money to Maury was causing trouble in their marriage. Jed admitted that he feared he might lose his son's affection if he withheld money. They talked for a long time, considering different ways to speak to Maury. For the first time in months, husband and wife shared a rapport with each other.

If parents cannot completely agree on matters concerning their children, they can consider some form of compromise or acceptance of one or the other's point of view. Snap judgments and unilateral decisions can be destructive. Obvious disagreement between parents forces a child to deal with divided loyalty.

Siblings and Money

Some parents bend over backward to keep things "fair" and "equal" among their children. Being fair, in the sense of being strictly equal, is impossible. If you try to give each child the same gift at the same time, you may lose sight of the fact that children have individual personalities, needs, and wishes. What you *can* do is give each child equal, individual consideration.

Linda, a young single woman, requested money from her parents for a down payment on a condominium. The parents were able and willing to give the money, but were concerned about the feelings of their older daughter, Debbie, who, with her husband, had bought a house some years before *without* the parents' help. Would Debbie be jealous if they gave Linda money? Should they give Debbie a like amount even though she didn't need it at this time?

The parents gave Linda the money. Because they wanted things out in the open, they told Debbie about their plans to help Linda. Debbie was happy for her sister, but even if her response had been different, the parents would have achieved their goal—an atmosphere of candor.

The principle of offering equal consideration—but not necessarily equal material gifts—can help you to be comfortable with giving as the occasion or situation arises. If it puts you more at ease, you can set aside a sum to use whenever you wish for each of your children. But a set amount of money does not always cover every situation. Care has to be taken that your efforts, no matter how well-intentioned, do not backfire and result in playing off one sibling against another.

In case of real need or emergency, all rules go out the window.

> Tony was in a car accident. He suffered internal injuries and needed several operations. The medical bills piled up, far exceeding his health insurance.
>
> Tony's parents didn't wonder about keeping things "fair." They paid some of his bills. "Your job," they said, "is to get well. Don't worry about money now."
>
> The other siblings also rallied around, one with money, and all with frequent hospital visits.

Comfort and emotional help and nurture come from sources other than just money. The best kind of help comes from *equal consideration* and individual *love*.

Bequests

No financial decision is more personal than deciding how to have your money distributed after you die. Depending on your wishes, you can leave the money to your children outright, or set up a system that distributes money at predetermined intervals.

Said one parent:

> "I worked hard for my money and I don't want it frittered away. I've devised a schedule of payments. It's a slow procedure, but I think it will give my children long-term security. Anyway, I'm pleased with it."

And another:

> "I had the fun of playing my game. My children will be able to enjoy the fruits of my labor any way they like."

Your will should be an accurate reflection of your intentions.

If you have not divided the money equally, be sure that the words say what you want them to.

Parents who favor one child over the other set up a voice—and a judgment—from the grave that will haunt the children in their later years, both the favored one and the one out of favor. Think long and hard before employing such tactics. The ghosts you leave behind can be far more powerful than the money.

In the case of an ill or handicapped child, financial plans can be discussed with all the siblings. Such discussions can foster feelings of closeness and solidarity, and the other children may very well feel relieved that financial arrangements have been made for the disabled child.

Capable legal counsel will help you to explore all existing avenues and insure against unnecessary complications. Wills should be reviewed and perhaps updated periodically. The financial world changes rapidly, and so do family situations, needs, and resources.

Harmony in a family stems from feelings of caring, dignity, and self-esteem. We can hope that any financial decisions would enhance and support those relationships rather than hinder or cripple them.

Ideally, parents want to see their adult children exercise individual strengths and abilities. We want to be helpful, without stifling our children's initiatives. We each have to decide what we *can* do and what we *wish* to do—there is no *must do*. More important than the issue of whether or not to be involved financially with adult children is the spirit in which the decision is made. If the decision is a reflection of love, acceptance, and respect, it will be right for that family.

Reflections

1. After you read each question, close your eyes, pause for a while, and give yourself time to remember events and experiences when you were a young adult.

- Think about the gifts you received from your parents. Did you ever feel that a gift was inappropriate? Why?
- How did you feel when you received a gift, however small, that was exactly what you wanted?
- How did you feel if your parents gave a gift to your brothers or sisters, but not to you? Or if they gave them "better" gifts?

- Think back to a time when you were negotiating with your parents about "spending money." How did you feel about yourself in these negotiations?
- What mistakes or unwise decisions did you make?
- Did you feel that your parents treated you fairly?

- Did your parents admonish you when you spent money purely for fun?
- Did your parents spend money for fun with you?
- Did you know you could get money from one parent for certain things the other parent would not allow?
- How did you feel about that?
- Did you feel more comfortable when your parents agreed about giving you or refusing you money?

- Did you ever borrow money from your parents?
- How did you feel when you paid it back, or did not pay it back?

- How much did you know about your parents' financial status?
- Did that knowledge or lack of it influence your assessment of how they treated you?

- If you inherited money or material gifts, how did you feel about the arrangements by which you received them?

- What does that tell you about how you would set up bequests?

2. Review each of the above situations, as if they were happening now, and put yourself in your child's place. Then, go back to the role of parent and compare your two reactions to the questions.
    - What is *similar* about the way your parents treated you and the way you treat your children?
    - What is *different* about the way your parents treated you and the way you treat your children?
    - Are you satisfied with the way you handle money?
    - Are there any changes you would like to make?

Chapter 4

When Your Grown Children Move Back Home

Margaret appeared on her parents' doorstep with her baby in her arms.

Craig returned home alone soon after his second wedding anniversary.

Marv lost his job. He and his family moved in with his parents.

Children grow up and move out. As parents, we think that we have completed a chapter in our lives. At first, we may feel lonely, even bereft, but most of us gradually experience a sense of freedom. Then—sometimes with advance notice, sometimes unexpectedly—the children are back on our doorstep.

Such homecomings occur frequently in today's climate of changing lifestyles and economic conditions. The homecoming can be happy, or jarring and disruptive. You may feel bewildered at first, then angry, then guilty because of the anger. You may be torn between wanting to resist the intrusion, and wanting to be a "good parent."

"Am I still responsible?" a parent may wonder. "Didn't I finish my job? Where did I fail?"

"I can't turn my back on my child who needs me. Other parents don't have this trouble. Why me?"

"My husband and I dreamed of selling the house and traveling when he retired. We can forget that now!"

"I never imagined I'd be faced with running a full house again. I didn't plan for it, and I don't know what my role is supposed to be."

The word *role* is a key here. Parents of young children have well-defined roles. Parents of adult children have roles that are ill-defined, and often not defined at all.

How do you deal with the problems that can arise when a grown-up child returns home? Some problems are simple to solve, others complex. How do you communicate with your children? How do you express your needs and wishes?

Look for Reasons for the Homecoming

Why do adult children return home? When parents understand the reasons for their children's moving back home, and analyze their own reactions, they will be better able to cope with the situation.

Some reasons are obvious: economic, educational, marital, geographic—circumstances that can cause young people to need a temporary stopover before gathering momentum for their true solo flight into the world.

Marv and his family came home because of a clear economic crisis. Margaret returned because of the end of her marriage and her poor financial status; she needed some comfort and financial help. Craig also came home for marital reasons. His situation looked more temporary than Margaret's; he told his parents that he was planning to look for a place of his own very soon.

What about problems that are less apparent, less tangible, problems that are not discussed because they are not fully understood? Some young people, no matter how adult chronologically, still have some growing up to do before they can face the world successfully. This can range from the need for a little last minute tender loving care, to increasing signs of overt or underlying psychological neediness. Sometimes this neediness is encouraged by the parents because of their own neediness.

Once the reason has been determined, steps can be taken to ease the adult child's transition back into—and out of—the family nest.

Reorganize the Household

Some of the incidents that cause trouble in a multigenerational household may be good material for a situation comedy, but they can be devastating for daily living.

One father, suffering dismay and discomfort with the arrival of his grown children, shared his grievances with us:

- "The phone is always busy."
- "The kitchen is never closed."
- "The noise level is always at a peak."
- "The baby never naps."
- "My chair is always occupied."
- "My wife and I have no time to talk to one another."

"Whose house is it, anyway?" he asked.

Families can avoid some of these upsets by addressing them immediately and openly. When anticipated and discussed, many of the irritations of daily life can be eliminated or reduced.

What you essentially have when parents and grown children live together is two families living in one space—even if one of the "families" consists of a single adult child, and the "space" is a large house. The first step to take is for everyone in the household to acknowledge that, although the children are back in the house, they are now adults, with the privileges and responsibilities that come with maturity. A new living arrangement is being established, one that requires mutual courtesy, consideration, *and* a new set of ground rules.

Without these rules, both you and your adult children may flounder, not knowing your roles or how to behave. You may find yourself walking on eggs in your own house, or becoming once again the parent you were when your children were little— giving them instructions on what to wear, when to go out, and when to return. You may never have meant to indulge in this kind of behavior now that they are grown, but because you are all in the same house you may find it hard to refrain from sinking back into old, unwanted habits.

The rules you draw up may be simple and few, or may fill a long sheet of paper. They may be informal or strict, a mere list or a virtual contract. Instead of rules, they may be called "guidelines." But, whatever they are called, and however drawn up, when entered into in a spirit of love and cooperation, they will add to everyone's comfort. If new annoyances or situations crop up, the list can be amended.

Before writing anything down, talk.

- First, discuss the physical arrangements with your spouse.
- Then, discuss them with your child. Be honest about your desires and needs.
- Discuss the fact that you are all adults, and that you all want to be treated as such.
- Discuss matters of privacy for all the members of the household, and how this privacy may be achieved.

Then, start your list.

- Decide the kind of rules or guidelines you want, specific or general.

- Put down everything you can think of. The list can be shortened later.
- Decide if you want rules about various household chores—who does what and when?
- Decide if you want rules about household standards.
- Decide if you want to discuss any plans your child may have for entertaining at home. Will these plans need additional rules, such as notifying the parents in advance, or deciding which room or rooms to use?

Discuss with your family which goals are possible to attain, and which need a little compromise. A happier atmosphere can be achieved when all the participants are realistic about their expectations.

Set a Time-Line

When Marv and his family came to live with Marv's parents, the older couple felt that their home had been invaded. The grandchildren, healthy and active, bounced in, danced through the living room, and landed in Grandpa Harry's chair. It did not take long for them to learn that the chair was "Grandpa Harry's space" and was out of bounds. Reclaiming his chair helped to give Harry back a piece of his territorial comfort. Many other such elementary problems had to be worked out. However, that was only part of the total picture. The main concern was to know how long this "invasion" was going to last.

Harry and his wife called a conference. Together, parents and children set up a time-line that aimed at Marv and his family once more being on their own. The parents could see ahead to an end of the inconveniences created by the overcrowded living conditions. In the meantime, they relaxed and enjoyed their grandchildren's antics and the company of Marv and his wife.

The more specific the time-line, the more successfully the parties can live under the same roof. If it becomes clear that the time-line is not going to be met, a brief extension may be offered. Or, the children, with or without the participation of the parents, can seek other living arrangements.

It is a good idea for parents to examine their own attitudes and behavior occasionally to make sure they are not sabotaging the time-line. ("Maybe you shouldn't take that apartment—it's so dark and small; stay here another few months.")

Above all, it's important to be honest and direct if there are difficulties caused by the child's staying more than the original time agreed upon. "It's been great having you here, but it's getting to be a little too much for us," or, "It's a little too hard on our pocketbook," are better responses than gritting your teeth over an arrangement you no longer wish to continue.

Humor can be helpful. You can remind your children that the checkout time is posted on every hotel room door!

Hold on to Your Lifestyle

Margaret's return with her young baby, following the breakup of her marriage, created tension within the family. Her mother had recently gone back to work as a librarian. She worried about the added responsibility of having her daughter and granddaughter living at home. Margaret's father was worried about the added financial burden his daughter's return created. Margaret's teenage sister was worried about how much baby-sitting she might be called upon to do.

The family talked about their concerns together and decided to maintain their individual lifestyles as much as possible. Margaret assumed many of the household chores and the major care of her baby. She enrolled in evening courses that would help to prepare her for a good job. The younger sister volunteered specific times for baby-sitting.

All members of this family felt that their lives were moving ahead despite Margaret's unplanned-for return.

Parents will be more comfortable if they maintain the new lifestyle they already enjoy, or go ahead with the plans they made when their children originally left home. Within the realm of reasonableness, such action will keep mother and father smiling and loving the children.

Nurture, but Don't Smother

Returning home can provide the young adult with a transition between school and career.

> Christina's parents welcomed her back home after graduation. She said she needed financial support during her transition from school to work. Shortly after her return, the parents became aware of Christina's real need—to test whether they were still "there" for her.
>
> They noticed that she was not quite comfortable living at home. On the one hand, she guarded her privacy; on the other, she seemed scared of being on her own. She seemed unsure about some of the important decisions she had to make.
>
> Her parents had mixed feelings, too. They had always been loving and supportive, but now they were unsure of themselves. Should they caution her against traveling alone at night; should they ask her to inform them when she would be home; should they question her about her various friends?

After talking things over with each other, Christina's parents decided to help their daughter grow into adulthood. They continued offering her the security and love she needed, all the while making a conscious effort to retain their newly established independent lifestyle and to encourage her to adopt her own independence. They avoided drawing Christina back into the cocoon of early childhood. They did not violate her privacy, meddle in her social plans, or ask for detailed reports. Christina did call them when she expected to be late and checked with them as to when it was convenient for her to entertain at home; these actions, her parents felt, were courtesies on their daughter's part rather than signs of neediness.

By treating Christina as an adult, her parents successfully provided the bridge she needed. They had avoided the all-too-familiar trap of resuming old familial roles—the strong parent and the helpless or clinging child or, conversely, the timid parent and the domineering child.

Christina grew in maturity, and her parents, no longer saddled with the responsibility of directing and controlling the activities of a child, experienced their own sense of freedom.

When a child goes away to college, a parent gets an education, too. Agnes learned an important lesson when her daughter, Polly, came home for a visit.

Polly paused in the entrance hall, her hand on the doorknob. A gentle beep of a car horn was heard from the driveway.

"There's Cal," said Polly. "We're going to the mall for pizza. Don't wait up, Mom. I'll see you in the morning."

Agnes looked up from the book she was reading. She saw Polly standing with one foot out the door, dressed in a sweater and jeans. Her hair was still wet from the shower she had been taking when Cal's phone call had interrupted her.

It was on the tip of Agnes' tongue to say, "You can't go out with your hair dripping wet like that. You'll catch your death of cold." She might have said that a few years ago, but there was much Agnes had learned since Polly had gone off to college. Having her come home for a visit was a wonderful treat. It was great to see her daughter growing up, and Agnes was growing up, too.

Agnes thought to herself, "When Polly's at school, I'm not there to see her when she goes out at eleven o'clock at night with wet hair. It's not up to me to comment on it when she's here. That's her business, not mine."

Agnes went back to reading her book.

If the returning child brings a spouse, the balance becomes extremely delicate. You must respect the relationship of two grown people who are sharing your home. They are now a couple and have a need for intimacy and privacy. Certainly you should turn a deaf ear to any marital squabbles—and above all, never take sides!

This last point cannot be emphasized too much:

- Don't take sides.
- Don't give an opinion.
- Walk out of the room.

Decide About Money

What place does money have when the adult child returns home? The child is usually in need of some kind of support, and often that support is financial. Parents' attitudes are important: Money is not being used merely as a commodity. It is entwined with self-esteem.

Does the child pay room and board—either fully or partly, or even in a token way? Will an extra mouth to feed strain the food budget? These are individual problems and decisions for each family.

As with all dealings with adult children, financial issues should be faced openly, truthfully, and lovingly. The adult child should not be made to feel inferior or inadequate.

Many of the aspects of money that were treated in an earlier chapter are helpful here.

Avoid Hanging On

Sometimes a grown child returns because of the demands of the parent.

> When Lucien's father died, his mother pleaded with him to "come home." He did so.
>
> A domineering woman, she demanded that Lucien give her not only financial security, but companionship as well.
>
> The mother controlled their social life, limiting it to Lucien's driving her to see family and her own friends. Lucien acquiesced out of his own compulsion to continue being "Mama's Good Boy."
>
> Lucien never married. Mother and son lived together until the mother's death. Lucien, then forty-five years old, had to reconstruct his life.

Had mother and son been more independent of one another, they would have had the opportunity to experience greater satisfaction in their individual lives. They might have chosen to live together, while still giving one another the gift of independence.

Although most people are not as controlling as Lucien's mother, we can all periodically review our relationships with our children to guard against destructive behavior.

Ask yourself some questions:

- Do you insist upon your grown children's participation in all or most of your own engagements?
- Do you expect to be included in all or some of your children's social life?
- Is your involvement with your children limiting your own, or their, experiences?
- Do you expect too frequent "weather reports" in your conversations with your children? About work? Home life? Relationships? Money?

If you suspect that you are becoming too intrusive in your children's lives, shift some of the focus to your own life. Expand and develop your own interests, and increase your social engagements with your own friends. It will be more fun!

Assume Responsibility for Your Own Life

When their daughter moved into her own apartment, Pete and Grace worried about how they were going to get along without her. Jill was their peacemaker, their referee. As soon as she moved out, they started to quarrel more than before.

Through phone calls and visits, Pete and Grace let their daughter know "what she had done to them" by moving out.

Jill felt anxious and guilty and finally moved back home. The parents continued bickering and Jill continued "refereeing," until the day that Jill looked at her parents and said it was time for all of them to stop this game. "I'm moving," she said. "You'll just have to resolve your problems by yourself. Maybe marriage counseling, maybe divorce."

Pete and Grace looked at each other in horror. When their daughter left, they started to talk to each other and admitted that they did not want a divorce. They had sunk into a comfortable pattern of bickering, a pattern made more comfortable by the continued presence of their daughter.

In this case, living together was serving no one. The family had fallen into a trap that was preventing them—parents and daughter alike—from growing up. How much better it would have been if, before this destructive relationship was formed, Pete and Grace had worked out their marital difficulties and encouraged Jill to get on with her own life.

Parents may truly intend to be welcoming and supportive when children return home, but intention alone is not enough. A family needs clarity of purpose and goals. If family members lack such direction, they are likely to spin their wheels and get stuck.

More questions to ask yourself:

- Do you bind your children to you by being needy?
- Do you make them feel guilty, consciously or unconsciously, for leaving you "all alone"?

Learn to recognize the signs that family development is being stunted.

- Is there no relief from bickering and arguing?
- Is there no movement on the part of the young adult in the outside world? In employment? In relationships?
- Is the adult child resistant to assuming greater responsibility for his or her own life?
- Are your and your spouse's plans remaining on the back burner?

If the answers to these questions are distressing, the family must look into removing the obstacles to progress. Some children need extra urging to leave the nest. Some parents need extra urging to push them out. Timeliness and appropriateness for such a push must be determined by the parents. Acting out of love, parents can set their children free without losing them.

Face Problems Head-on

Nobody ever said that living together is easy. It is *hard* to set the rules for living together, and it is *hard* to set a time-line for your children's departure. You may feel guilty and inhospitable. You may also be fearful of losing your children's love. How do you deal with this?

- Acknowledge your feelings.
- Resolve that the long-term goal of a good relationship is most important.
- Think over what you want to say.
- Rehearse it.
- Steel yourself, if necessary.
- Say it with love.

There are abnormal and extreme situations, such as drug addiction, severe emotional disorders, or criminal behavior, for which professional help is necessary. Sometimes a child is not capable of being independent and cannot live at home in safety and comfort. The parents have a responsibility to protect their own lives, those of their other children, and the community. In such circumstances, the parents, however unhappily and reluctantly, have to find a suitable supportive environment away from home for their child.

Guidance may be sought from the clergy, community counseling agencies, and government social services. Helpful materials can be obtained from nearby libraries and universities.

The return home of grown children can create stress. To minimize the pain and maximize the rewards, keep in mind these guidelines:

- Maintain respect for one another.
- Support one another.
- Keep your sense of humor.

Reflections

1. After you read each question, pause for a while and give yourself time to remember events and experiences when you were a young adult.

- Recall a time when you came home, thinking of yourself as a grown-up, and you felt that your parents treated you as a child.
- Were you upset? What did your parents say or do that upset you?

- Think of a time when you were a young adult and you experienced a failure.
- What was your parents' attitude toward you? And toward the failure?

- Think of a time, while in your parents' home, that you felt your privacy was not respected.
- How would you have liked the situation to have been handled?

2. Now, go back to each reflection and imagine your child answering these same questions.

Exercises

1. Divide a piece of paper into two columns.

   In one column, write a list of rules that you would expect house guests to observe.

   In the other column, write a list to be observed by children returning home.
   - How are the two lists the same?
   - How are they different?
   - What would you like to change?
   - What does looking at the two lists side by side reveal to you?
   - Are you expecting too much or too little from your children?

2. If your grown child has come home to live, can you identify the reason or reasons for the return?
   - Is there "unfinished business" to be resolved?

- Would you like to set a time-line for departure?
- Are there signs that things are at an impasse?

3. Would you like to change the situation at home?
   - What changes would you like to see come about?
   - What action should you take?
   - What changes must you ask your children to make?
   - Can you and your children bring about these changes alone, or should you seek professional help?

Chapter 5

Celebrating Holidays and Other Occasions

As things change in this stage of our lives, the holidays change, too. Sometimes conscious effort is required to assure that although the celebration may be different, it can still be joyful.

Ask people for an impression of a happy family holiday and most answers will stress a large laughing group clustered around a table. Polished wood or white formica, gracious dining room or crowded kitchen, filet mignon or spaghetti and meatballs—each family has its own image of being together, eating together, and laughing together.

People speak not only of a holiday but of their anticipation of it. Valerie told us that she "draws pictures" in her mind a week before the big event.

> "I see Wendy and Beth off in a corner, talking about their new beaus. I hear laughter in the living room where the boys are exchanging jokes.
>
> "Through the kitchen window, I see a Frisbee sail by. I hear the sound of a guitar upstairs, the sound of footsteps in the hall. I smell wonderful aromas from the kitchen."

A different situation, but a similar outpouring of happiness, was described by Alicia, recently divorced.

"I can't tell you how excited I was, just knowing that Sandy was going to spend the holiday with me. I couldn't wait for the doorbell to ring. But I have to admit that I was nervous. Here I was in a small apartment, after our big house, and after the divorce. Would Sandy feel funny?

"At the same time, though, I knew it would be a good day. I had bought tickets to the show we both wanted to see; I had made reservations at a charming new restaurant; I couldn't wait to hear about Sandy's recent move; I couldn't wait to talk about my new job. I just knew it would work out well. And guess what—it sure did!"

There are many ways to celebrate the same occasion. As life goes on and the years bring changes, we can find these new ways. We are limited only by our own imaginations.

Why We Need Holidays

Everybody needs celebrations. Primitive peoples devised various rituals, first to control whatever forces they thought were shaping their lives, and then to keep the tribe and the family together.

These festive interludes in our lives help to keep us together. They fuse the past with the present, giving us a precious sense of continuity.

Holidays are an opportunity for family feelings to be expressed and expanded. We wish for warm and wonderful experiences to build a bank of memories for our children to carry into future life, and to establish and strengthen a mature relationship between children and parents.

Ritual and ceremony enrich us. More than a pleasurable luxury, a holiday gives our lives individual definition. The entire country may eat turkey on Thanksgiving, but only in our house, only in our family, are there Grandma's pecan stuffing and apple tarts; only at our house are there special jokes, special stories, and special people. Personal holiday traditions evolve through the years. Then, just at the point when everything seems flawless—in our memories, that is—the children grow up and the holidays change.

The Holidays of Yesterday: Remembering How They Looked

"We used to cram twenty people into this room," said Eugene. "Now the old folks are gone and the children live all over the country. My wife and I sit at the table and stare at each other."

"When the kids were little," said Hilda, "there were more dishes for Thanksgiving dinner than you could count. Oysters, chowder, turkey, pies—you name it, we had it. Those days are gone. Who has the time or strength for it anymore, even when the kids do come home? But I miss those dinners."

Yes, we miss the holidays of the past, and sometimes we want them back, intact and unchanged. Obviously, we cannot have them back that way. Nothing stays the same through the years— not we, not our children, not our circumstances, not even something as rockribbed and sacred as the celebration of Thanksgiving, a holiday that comes with its own classic props: *Food*—turkey, sweet potatoes, cranberry sauce. *Backdrop*—a table surrounded by friendly, caring people sharing a joyous occasion. *Activities*—football and the parade on television, stories and jokes around the fireplace, Ping Pong in the playroom. This is the prototype of the perfect Thanksgiving in many people's minds.

As to our own *actual* holidays, the years soften our recollections, and even distort them. Those perfect holidays were probably not completely perfect. Tempers flared then, as they do today, rivalries were displayed, people had last-minute emergencies that kept them from showing up, the baby came down with the flu, Uncle Walter always fought with Aunt May about politics.

Although those holidays cannot be *duplicated* (and sometimes it is just as well!), the happy sentiments that those gatherings engendered can be revived.

Start with some memories.

- Summon up the old holidays in your mind. Think about them without sorrow or longing. Enjoy your thoughts.
- Think about the good things—the house smelled wonderful, the table looked inviting, the children clamored to tell the story of the first Thanksgiving.
- Think of other things, little annoyances and hardships. More than turkey simmered in the house. When Uncle Walter and Aunt May started their political "discussions," half the table joined in and took sides. The children, as they grew older, refused to talk about the Pilgrims; no amount of coaxing could persuade them. And what about the host or hostess? You worked for days on the feast and afterward were faced with a gigantic cleanup.
- Return to the good memories—no sense dwelling on the not-so-good. Besides, Uncle Walter and Aunt May always made up by the time the coffee was poured.

The Holidays of Today: How They Look Now

The table is set, the lights are lit, the people are seated. But wait, something is awry. The room is different, the food is different, the people are different—someone is missing, someone is added.

"My daughter's in Denver, my son's in Pittsburgh—and neither can come home for Thanksgiving. They're too busy right now. They'll be home for Christmas. At least I hope so."

"My son wants to bring his live-in girlfriend home for the holidays. I don't know. Holidays are for families, not outsiders. Besides, my father-in-law is pretty touchy that they're not married yet."

"When my husband was alive, half the time I made the dinner and half the time we were invited out. I don't make dinners anymore, and when I am invited out I feel like an extra."

Change is part of everyone's life; coping with change is everyone's responsibility. At this present juncture in our lives, change seems to come with increasing rapidity:

Distance. The children are scattered all over the country.
Loss. Friends and family members become ill and die.
Tighter budgets. We prepare for retirement; we learn to live on retirement income.
Changes in the family. The family does not always shrink; sometimes it expands. The in-laws acquired when our children marry can add pleasure to our lives or bring problems.

Start the Holiday of Tomorrow: Create a Daydream

At the start of this chapter, we wrote about Valerie, who described the "pictures" she drew in her head in anticipation of a holiday.

Building upon Valerie's method, a great way to set the stage for a happy holiday is to create a daydream of what is, for you, a perfect occasion. Make the daydream as sharp and clear as an architect's blueprint. Include the various sights, sounds, smells, and emotions of your ideal celebration. Include also the setting, the guests, the food, the after-dinner activities—plus your role. Active participant? Spectator? A little of each?

The daydream of an ideal holiday is not necessarily a resurrection of the past. It can bridge a time gap, taking what was good with the old holiday, combining what is good with the present holiday, and adding a new fillip or two.

- Choose a quiet place to create the dream. Sit back, relax. Are you comfortable?
- Take as much time as you wish for fashioning the daydream.
- What you dream about need not look like any real celebration you have ever attended.
- Or, it may be very much as you remember holidays when the children were young.
- Visualize the setting—your home, someone else's, a restaurant? Colors—bright, subdued? Decoration—familiar, different?
- Visualize the cast of characters. Immediate family only, other family members? Old friends, new acquaintances?
- What is everyone doing? Your role, other people's?
- Are you having fun?
- Are you surprised at what you see?

To give your daydream extra dimension, enlarge it. Visualize an elaborately designed holiday store window, a display with scenery and moving figures—right out of Disneyland. Visualize the people talking and laughing. What are they talking about? Why are they laughing? They are having fun. Can you visualize yourself having as much fun during your holiday, too?

Compare the daydream to your present life. Then, with the dream still in your mind, conjure up another blueprint, one that considers the present physical and emotional circumstances of your family.

Your Role Is Different

We talked with several people who had trouble adjusting to a change of situation—and, consequently, to a new role. Their time-honored place in life, that of being the leader, the person in full charge, seemed to them to have been pushed a bit into the background, while their children, or children's spouses, took over. Lynne told us that when she goes to her married daughter's house for Thanksgiving she feels left out.

"They always used to come to us," said Lynne, "but last year their kids were sick and the year before that they were too young to travel. It's not that I feel strange there. It's more like I've been—not replaced, exactly, but moved aside. Shoved aside is more like it. Do you know what a *sous chef* is? That's what I feel like. The assistant chef. The under chef. Not the main one anymore."

Many parents acknowledge, accept, and even welcome the independent lifestyles of their adult children. And then—along comes Christmas. Everyone arrives home to the familiar house, to the familiar smells of good cooking, and to the familiar roles of bygone years. Suddenly, old feelings and old dialogues creep back. The oldest daughter is once again the big sister bossing her younger sister and brother around, the youngest child slips into being the pampered baby of the house, and the mother finds herself saying things like, "You're wearing hiking boots? On Christmas Day?"

Many parents had stories like this to relate.

"In our home, holidays used to be a time to watch your step and count your words," said Terry. "I would give myself warnings the day before—don't say this, don't say that. Two years ago, we were going to my daughter's for our first Easter dinner there. I had given myself so many warnings that I was completely befuddled and even a little angry.

"My poor daughter didn't know what was wrong with me when I called her at seven o'clock that morning, and in this loud, crazy voice, shouted, 'Don't forget to baste the ham midway through—and keep on basting!'

"To make sure she knew who was boss, I kept repeating it. 'Don't forget to baste the ham!'

"As soon as I put back the receiver, I asked myself why on earth I did such a stupid thing. It sounded so much like her old high school days when I was constantly nagging, 'Don't forget your notebook—your keys—your lunch—your head!'

"When we arrived at our daughter's house, I apologized about it and made a little joke. I'm more relaxed since then, but I'm still a little on my guard."

The Holiday Setting May Be Different

When the traditional setting of the holiday changes, many people feel as Lynne did—left out. Raymond felt this way, too, and more.

"A guest is not the host," Raymond told us. "My wife feels the same way. She's always complaining that my daughter-in-law is a terrible cook and shouldn't attempt anything more complicated than a plain, *unstuffed* turkey. To tell the truth, my daughter-in-law's not a bad cook. I'm beginning to think it's us. I think we just want the holidays in our own house, the way they used to be. The way they should be."

Is there ever a "should be"? Does time ever stand still? Are we owed a "rightful place"? Are we, or anyone else, able to make up *all* the rules, *all* the time?

Lynne expressed her feelings about the holidays: in her child's house she feels like a *sous chef*, the second in command; she feels left out. Raymond feels similarly left out, but because of his frankness about his and his wife's resistance to change, he may be on the way toward letting go of some of the control he used to have.

Paulette—equally frank, and very much on top of whatever changes life might bring her—had to alter not only her ideas of what constituted a Christmas holiday, but her own role as well. She called her new attitude her "conversion."

"It finally hit me," said Paulette, "that the fruit cakes and the mince pies and the thousands of cookies I baked all those years—and I want you to know that I grumbled over every one of them—were a kind of insurance for me. Those cakes told me that I was still young and still needed, and, more important, that my home was still the holiday center for the family.

"I realized this when my daughter told me she wanted everyone to come to *her* house for Christmas. She also told me that *she* would do the baking. I was very upset, really seething, until I sat down and thought the whole thing out.

"This happened over five years ago, and I've enjoyed myself ever since. There are times when my daughter or my daughters-in-law do the baking, and times when I do it. Sometimes we go to their houses, and sometimes they come to ours. Lately it has dawned on me that I really do enjoy the holidays when I come as a 'guest.' I enjoy the lack of responsibility, and also the extra free time to play with my grandchildren."

Some people do not mind a change of setting, but are faced with the problem of *which* setting to choose. Jane, with three married children, spoke of Thanksgiving as her "yearly dilemma."

"Christmas is easy," Jane said. "We·have open house Christmas Eve *and* Christmas Day, so there's plenty of time for everyone to come and go whenever it's convenient for them.

"But Thanksgiving is a one-shot deal. All our children have in-laws. There is constant inviting back and forth. It's the same questions every year. Who comes to us? Where do we go? One year two of our children each invited us, and the third one wanted to come here.

"My husband said it's getting to be like Russian Roulette. Someone is bound to get hurt."

Other people were faced with the Thanksgiving dilemma. Most solved it by planning in advance and by making friendly "deals" with their children and their children's in-laws, whereby they shared the holiday or took turns. The ones with the most success were those who were able to speak openly with all the members of their family. Once the situation is aired, the family can work together to find a solution that satisfies everyone—a "win-win" situation.

The Cast of Characters May Be Different

When a child lives far away and can't come home, or a spouse or dear relative has died, it's natural to feel forlorn, even unconnected.

Harriet and Brad were faced with a lonely Passover. Their son was to be in Europe on business; their daughter and son-in-law would be visiting his family in California.

"We decided to invite some of our friends whose children would also be away," said Harriet.

"Two weeks before Passover, Brad got this brilliant idea. We took four o'clock in the afternoon as the standard and told everyone to write down the comparable time where their children were going to be. We all told our children that we would toast them at exactly four o'clock, our time, and that they should do the same wherever they were.

"It turned out to be just lovely. At exactly four o'clock, we raised our glasses and said a prayer for all our kids, for their good health and safe return. Later, we sat down to eat and began to talk about when they were little. What a day. Everybody had a funny story to tell."

New faces at the table—your children's friends or in-laws— can cause a strain on family intimacy and closeness.

Arthur mentioned that of the three sets of his children's in-laws, he and his wife got along with two of them very well.

"Our oldest child's in-laws," Arthur said, "are another story. The man's a boor, and his wife—I swear that woman keeps score. '*We* brought this last time, *you* bring it this time.'

"They dominate the whole day. Everybody has to do what they want to do and talk about what they want to talk about. It's gotten so bad that my wife and I are thinking of finding some excuse for not being with our family next year."

Such a situation requires tact and diplomacy at the holiday table, and soul-searching questions at home.

- Which will please me more—to have a holiday with my family, including the disliked in-laws, *or* to avoid seeing the disliked in-laws, which might very well mean giving up seeing my family?
- Am I willing to accept these people for the redeeming features of the occasion?
- Do I want to risk causing a rift between my child and my child's spouse and in-laws?

The unpleasant in-laws can be treated in the same manner other such people are treated, be they relatives or friends—with courtesy, tolerance, and patience. Each case, each personality, is different. You can decide which "treatment" to give them. You can also learn to ignore them.

The Whole Holiday Is Different

If you really try, you can find fault with anything. With some of the old familiar props gone, the holiday can be—if you allow it—disappointing. Because there is no piano in your child's house, will there be no singing of all the old songs? Because there is no fireplace in your new apartment, will there be no clustering around the warmth of the flames; hence, will there be no spirited conversation? Such losses may seem trivial to some, vital to others.

Lest we get too mired in nostalgia, we should not forget that many of us have no wish to relive either part or all of the old holidays. For one reason or another, many people are eager to welcome a new way of celebrating. Daniel was only too happy to rid himself of old memories.

"Before my divorce," said Daniel, "every holiday was a nightmare. My wife sulked through the whole day, the children were bewildered and bad-tempered, and I guess I wasn't exactly the life of the party either.

"Now, would you believe it, since my wife and I have both remarried, we each have great times. We're both willing to share the children, and take turns.

"Those of us who are not together call each other and everyone is satisfied."

Sometimes the tables are turned, and it is the parents who have a sudden opportunity to do something new, something that does not include their children. Matt told us that last Easter he and his wife were offered the chance to go on a cruise to Bermuda.

"It was a fantastic package," said Matt, "a real steal. Dotty and I were wild to go. But we didn't know how to tell the kids. We always have the whole crowd every year. Would they feel rejected?

"In the end, we just told them, 'No beating about the bush!' They were very understanding. As understanding, I figured out later, as we were when they would tell us they couldn't come home from college for Thanksgiving."

With a look of pleasurable surprise, Matt added, "The kids were so happy for us, so glad we were taking the cruise, that we doubly enjoyed our vacation."

From Fantasy to Reality: The Daydream Becomes Real

Go back to the perfect daydream. It may be rooted in reality, as were Valerie's "mind pictures," it may bear no resemblance to today's reality at all, or it may be a little of both.

As objectively as you can, decide how much of the daydream can be translated into today's reality, and how much cannot. Even if parts cannot be re-created literally, if they're worthy of the dream and prompt good memories, it is possible to sustain these memories and transform them into a new kind of warmth and joy.

Be realistic. It is not a matter of lowering your expectations, but of acknowledging and accepting the changes, and anticipating, with pleasure and a sense of adventure, new circumstances and new ideas. Rather than dwelling on how things have changed, and how nothing can match the good old days, employ the positive word: *choice*. A choice of alternatives awaits. Just as we all dress, eat, and think differently than we did ten or fifteen years ago, so are our holidays certain to be different.

Aim for New Ideas, New Designs, New Holidays

Transporting the good feelings and emotions from the daydream in your mind into your home or dining room (or someone else's dining room) is easier than it might seem.

Judy and Stan told us how, without too much effort, they changed the whole tenor of their holiday.

"There we were," said Judy, "ready to go down to the basement and drag up the bridge table and all the extra chairs. I said something about hating the fact that we had to turn the dining table around so that both tables could be put together and stretched through half the living room.

"Stan looked at me and said, 'You know what I hate—I hate turkey.'

"One thing led to another, and before we knew it, we decided to forget the bridge table, leave the dining table alone, and have a buffet!

"It turned out to be a huge success. My daughter brought her lasagna, I made goulash, and Stan picked up a couple of pounds of sliced turkey at the deli—to keep the die-hards happy.

"We've eaten many a Thanksgiving feast in our lives, but I don't think any of us will ever forget that one. We're already talking about fried chicken and baby back ribs for next year."

Your daydream provided your ideal picture of a holiday. Now whittle it down to size.

- Think about the old holiday—which parts to keep and which parts to change.
- Discuss your plans with other family members.
- Be conscious of necessary changes and adaptations.
- Welcome various changes. Instead of grieving for the old roles and surroundings, take pleasure in the new.
- Consider including aged relatives. They can enrich the occasion.
- Be aware of your children's needs. Career commitments and other facets of their new status may interfere with their coming home at this time.

In talking to parents about the holidays, we kept hearing about the tremendous efforts many of them made in order to be noncontrolling. Many parents told their children that "it's up to you if you want to come home."

Marie said that she used to say the same thing, but gradually realized that it was not in the best interest of the family.

"Subconsciously," said Marie, "I knew I was giving my children too much of a burden. I was forcing them to make a difficult choice. If they came home, I wondered if they were doing so to satisfy me. If they didn't come home, I was afraid I was making them feel guilty.

"I've learned to let go. I just say, 'Sure, I'd love to have you come home. If it's possible for you, fine. If not, let's plan for another time.'

"I think saying this has done a lot to make us more relaxed with each other."

If some parents still cling to their former roles of parenting small children, others go to the opposite end of the spectrum with, "It's time *you* took over the holidays; I've done it long enough." Both kinds of behavior demean and belittle the adult child. With a little forethought you can avoid these traps.

- Avoid dumping the total responsibility for the holiday on adult children who may not yet have the resources—physical, emotional, or financial—to cope.
- Make way for the new generation. Encourage your children to participate in, or take charge of, some of the holiday preparations.
- Accept graciously their contributions to the celebration. Take pride in their accomplishments, and compliment them.
- Overlook what you feel are shortcomings. Concentrate on enjoying the camaraderie.

- Blend your children's ideas with your traditions. You will be paving the way for a new understanding and rapport, and you will have a richer holiday.

When you're the guest, try to suspend your judgment as to the "proper" trappings of the holiday. Larry recalled a holiday he and his wife had spent at their married son's house.

"Our son brought out a platter with this enormous baked fish, complete with head and tail.

"I heard a hiss in my ear. Irene was whispering, and none too softly. '*Fish*? for *Thanksgiving*?'

" 'Sh-h-h! You know they're vegetarians. And this is their house and their choice. ' "

Rethink the Holiday: Attitudes

Some planning and effort can preserve the festive spirit.

- Drop from your vocabulary, and your mind, negative words and thoughts: "When I think of what used to be, I could cry." "The holidays are so much work. How will I get it all done?"
- Add positive words and thoughts: "Let's start some new customs." "Whatever we do this year, let's have fun."
- If you do not want to recapture the old days, think about what you do want to change.

Maxine wanted a whole new look for her holiday.

"When I was a child, we always spent Thanksgiving at my grandparents' house and, in later years, at my parents' house. My grandmother and mother both reveled in being the cooks and nurturers for the whole family, the total providers of food and comfort.

"My grandfather and father, on the other hand, were the patriarchs. Everything was handed to them. They had nothing to do but sit back and be served.

"My husband and I are not comfortable with those roles. We both want to enjoy the holiday. We talked it over with our children, and now every Thanksgiving we go to a different restaurant. It has worked out very well."

What if the rest of the family resists change? Apply the old watchwords—talk, talk, talk. Plan, negotiate, compromise. Take turns in choosing various aspects of the holiday. Some people alternate houses and styles of celebrating, agreeing to accept the choice of the current hostess.

Reorganize the Holiday: "Mechanics"

- Too busy to cook and plan? Ask other members for ideas and cooperation. Take advantage of modern conveniences— frozen food, takeout food, microwave ovens. Ask someone else to bake the pies, or buy them.
- Overwhelmed at the thought of planning a big celebration? Share these thoughts with your family. Tell them you're burdened by too much to do, and resentful when you're left alone in the kitchen. Ask for suggestions.
- Lonely or falling into self-pity because:
    The kids cannot come home? Arrange to call them on the telephone; plan some of the conversation in advance; concentrate on happy words.
    Your spouse is no longer alive? With your children, recall the happy times when your spouse was alive. Rekindle those memories; laugh and smile and feel good.
    You cannot afford a sumptuous feast—what will people think? Organize a pot luck dinner and ask everyone to bring a different dish.
    Your new condominium is too small? Copy Judy's idea,

and plan a buffet. Pillows on the floor can substitute for extra chairs.

The family has grown too large for one house? Divide into groups for separate dinners in separate houses and meet later in one house for dessert.

Redo the Holiday: The Old Groove Can Become New

- Replay in your mind the good parts of the "old tapes," all the good aspects of past holidays. Plan ways to bring back *some* of them.
- If there's no piano, ask everyone for suggestions; someone is bound to have a guitar or a harmonica. Or a kazoo! Even without a musical instrument, you can still sing your songs. Call your singing a cappella, and feel very professional about the whole thing.
- Buy plenty of film, arrange everyone on and around the sofa, have them all smile and wave, and then aim your camera and press the button. Voilá! New memories.
- Rituals and traditions—keep some, drop others, introduce new ones.

Recognize the old danger spots, and plan ways to avoid them. We mentioned previously that no sooner do some families get together than all the old roles and rivalries come to the fore. A way to minimize this is to be aware of your own behavior and hope that the adult children will follow suit. Also, by introducing new rituals and traditions, you may be able to break some of the old "spell."

Just as you wish sometimes to be able to stretch the walls in your house at holiday time, so do you need to stretch your imagination. There is no one right way to do anything.

When Henry's son had to be in another city the week of Thanksgiving in order to deliver an address, his parents postponed their family celebration of the holiday.

"I asked my son," said Henry, " 'How do we know exactly when the Indians and Pilgrims sat down together to their feast? What difference does it make what the date is for our gathering as long as we're together?'

"My son went off to honor his commitment, and the whole family enjoyed a wonderful feast two weeks later."

Work With New Roles and Circumstances in a Positive Way

- If you're a guest, don't take over. Enjoy the luxury of being a guest.
- If you find yourself without any plans:

    Take responsibility to make your holiday happy and cheerful.

    Make a conscious effort to have a holiday as much to your own liking as possible.

    Give of yourself to others, both physically and mentally. You will be pleasantly rewarded.

    Invite a friend or neighbor who is also alone for dinner.

    Find someone with whom to share the day—a friend, an acquaintance, or a business contact. Have dinner at your house, your friend's house, or a restaurant.

    Volunteer to work with people who need help.

    If you're alone, plan your holiday with the same detailed care you use for company. Good food and a good book or television program can provide lots of comfort. Draw the curtains, turn the lights down low, listen to good music, think good thoughts of yesterday, plan good things for tomorrow—and enjoy!

In whatever situation you find yourself, a positive device to employ is to remember your daydream. If you take even one tiny segment of the daydream and turn it into reality, you'll be enhancing your present holiday.

The important point to remember is that you want to savor and preserve the good feelings of the past and bring them into the present. Feelings are important, format less so. Remember, too, that each holiday is an opportunity for a clean slate, a new beginning, and new ideas.

Reflections

1. An outsider attending a family occasion witnesses a microcosm of the familial relationship. Imagine yourself in the dual roles of regular participant at your family's holiday celebration, plus that of outsider: an outsider who is magically *invisible*.
   - Try to be objective—you are the stranger describing your actions.
   - Analyze your behavior. Analyze your motivation. Were you trying to safeguard a family tradition, or control the celebration—and your children?
2. After you have "watched" yourself in an objective way, ask yourself some questions:
   - Do you always want to be the host?
   - Do you insist on continuing traditional annual patterns or are you willing to be flexible on all aspects of the holiday?
   - Do you insist that all the family members be present at every holiday celebration? Do you "make a fuss" if someone cannot come? Are you willing to accept your children's decisions to spend the holiday elsewhere?
   - When the children do come home, are you prepared for old sibling rivalries to surface?
   - Do you find yourself falling into old patterns—telling the children how to set the table, etc?
   - Are you willing to cope with unresolved family issues if they arise? Would you rather "sweep them under the rug" and enjoy the day for its own sake?
   - Are you willing to accept your children's styles of religious observance or nonobservance?

- Are you willing to allow the formation of separate relationships within the family that do not include yourself?
- Are you willing to give others the opportunity for a dialogue to reach an agreement?
- Are you willing to give thoughtful response to requests to bring additional guests to the celebration?
- Are you allowing for input from others?
- Are you leaving room in the daydream for parts of the holiday to be different from what you imagined?
- As a young adult, did you feel *obligated* to spend a holiday with your parents or family—even when circumstances made it difficult for you to do so?

Exercises

1. Describe your expectations for your children at holiday time. Are you willing to let go of some of these expectations?
2. Describe a disappointment involving a family holiday. Devise ways to let go of that disappointment.
3. Describe a marvelous family holiday you experienced in the past. Frequently visualize that occasion and recapture the happiness of the day.

Chapter 6

Weddings: Fun or Frenzy?

It is the eve of Susan's wedding, and her parents have gone to bed. Her father is already drifting into sleep, but her mother is restless.

Suddenly, she pushes her husband, and says in a loud voice, "I know Rick's a nice boy, but is he good enough for our Susan?"

Her husband opens one eye and mumbles, "No one is good enough for our Susan. Go back to sleep."

Weddings! What other celebration can foster so much anticipation and such anxious moments? Of all the rituals in our lives, the weddings of our children are usually the most eagerly awaited and planned for.

Weddings can give us the joy of seeing our children about to become happily established. They are a way to officially introduce the new couple to family and friends. The culmination of many parents' dreams, weddings can give us a sense of completion in our role of child-rearing. "As soon as I heard the 'I do's,' " one woman told us, "I felt the satisfaction of a job completed."

As with other rituals of society, weddings have undergone

various changes through the last few decades. In planning our own weddings, most likely we followed the conventions of preceding generations. The minute we got engaged, we ran to the shelf for the etiquette book. How comforting that book was! It gave explicit instructions for everything, from who pays for the music to the proper attire for the various members of the bridal party.

But even when courtship and marriage customs were more rigid and structured than they are now, many exceptions prevailed. Wartime played havoc with prescribed rules. And families, at various times and on all levels of economic strata, have bent the old rules and devised new ones. People from different parts of the country follow their own established customs.

During the free and easy—and often intense—times of the "hippies" and student revolts, weddings became relaxed and freewheeling. Informal dress, vegetarian or ethnic food, and the marriage service itself all served to infuse new life into old rituals. Whether or not these ideas are incorporated into today's weddings is irrelevant. The real lesson they gave to social behavior is that the most important people at the wedding are the people who are getting married. Rules, traditional or new, are helpful as long as we do not follow them in slavish fashion.

Setting the Stage

Weddings probably are one of the oldest rituals known to civilization, but to the participants and their families, each wedding is new, each one different. As with holiday celebrations, feelings take precedence over format. The young couple's comfort, and that of their families, is the chief concern.

Planning a child's wedding can be a joy. It can also create stress.

Edie described the weeks before her daughter's wedding.

"If ever there was a nervous wreck, it was me," said Edie. "I worried about everything—were our clothes formal enough, was the catering hall good enough, would everyone be happy with their table arrangements?

"When my husband told me to calm down, that the wedding would be as nice as any other wedding, I started thinking about other weddings. And then I remembered my cousin's son's wedding.

"It took place in a shabby hotel. The ceremony was very brief, and we could hardly hear any of it. The reception room was small and crowded and hot. The food was just so-so.

"But, do you know what? It was wonderful to see my relatives again. We all laughed and reminisced about the old days. And the bride and her family were very friendly and cordial. We had one of the best times ever!

"After thinking about that day, I stopped worrying about my daughter's wedding."

Choosing the bride's dress or deciding on the flowers to be used may be of great importance to some, less important to others. What is fundamental and basic to the marriage is the joining of two people and the spirit of the occasion.

A wedding unites two people; it also brings together two families. Suddenly, you are presented with a new set of people who will play a large part in your child's life. They may also play a large part in your life. You may not have met your child's future in-laws yet and are nervous at the prospect. You may have met them and disliked them or felt uncomfortable with them.

If this has happened, ask yourself why you dislike them:

- Are your feelings masking the fact that you do not like or approve of your child's future spouse?
- Are you uncomfortable with your child's interaction with the new family?

- Are you resentful of the other family's familiarity with your child?
- Are you perhaps a tiny bit jealous at now having to share your child, or at seeing your child give filial respect to another family, or at hearing your child call someone else— a perfect stranger—"Mom" or "Dad"?
- Are you fearful that your child is forming new loyalties and no longer will be as close to you?

Think about your desires for your child, and how your attitudes and behavior will affect those desires.

- Ask yourself what will result from such feelings and actions.
- Realize that your unfriendly behavior can cause difficulties for the young couple and, hence, your child. Is this what you want?
- Think of the difficulties you will be causing yourself. Realize that your unfriendliness may very well alter or diminish your relationship with your child.

Try to overcome, or modify, any negative feelings or actions.

- Think of ways to soften your behavior if up to now you have been withholding love and approval from the young couple. A friendly telephone call, some jokes, or a spontaneous invitation for lunch can lighten the atmosphere. Friendliness often begets more friendliness.
- Use these suggestions to help promote good feelings with the other family. You don't have to become instant buddies, nor do you have to like everything about them in order to share a friendly relationship with them. Include them in some family activities.
- Keep uppermost in your mind the goal of promoting your child's happiness.
- Realize that nobody is perfect.

If your child is accepted, welcomed, and valued by the new family, not only can you feel pleased, but you can also pat yourself on the back: "I'm glad I'm happy about this. My first thought is for my child's happiness."

On the other hand, if you see that the new family is not as welcoming as you would wish, try to offer the young people as comfortable a relationship as possible—without criticizing the other family.

Recognizing Different Perceptions, Different Dreams

Historically in our society, the wedding is the province of the bride's family. The bride and her parents decide on the size, style, and location of the wedding. What if the parents want one kind of wedding and the bride wants another? What if the groom or his family want a completely different kind? One set of parents wants a large formal party, the other a small garden party at home.

If the bride's family's wishes differ sharply from those of the groom's, both families can meet and talk things over. Maybe the wedding plans will not be changed, but a spirit of goodwill can be created.

- Discuss the plans with the young couple. Listen to their ideas. Tell them your own ideas.
- Discuss these plans with the other parents.
- Aim for arriving at mutually agreeable choices.
- Be frank about your financial situation.
- Be sensitive to the other parents' feelings.
- Keep your own ideas and plans, but be understanding and respectful about theirs.
- Don't be embarrassed to say no. Say it graciously.
- Be aware if disagreement stems from differences in background and try to work around these differences.
- Let go of being "right." Aim for a mutual pleasing of one another.

- Don't set up opposite "camps." Look for a "win-win" situation.
- Talk things over, keep a positive attitude, and treat other people's ideas with respect.
- Joyfully accept a supportive role if the *couple* want to make the wedding.
- Lighten up. Remember, this is a celebration!

The ceremony also needs to be planned. If there are religious or cultural differences between the young couple, and even if there are not, it must be decided well beforehand about the type of ceremony, where it will take place, and who will officiate.

The same principles of a positive attitude combined with respect for the other family apply when you are the parent of the groom. If you want a large wedding and the bride's family does not, or if your guest list has to be sharply reduced, you can plan to have a reception for your own family and friends after the wedding. If the wedding is shaping up to be very different from your old dreams, examine the differences. Are they really of such magnitude? Ask yourself if you're being influenced by, "What will my friends say?"

Clifford, a man of conventional habits, told us that he and his wife were quite apprehensive before their son's wedding.

"We liked our son's fiancée from the start," said Clifford, "but we were nervous when we met her family. One brother has a beard as wide as his shoulders. The other brother wears an earring. The whole family is very theatrical. How would we ever introduce them to our guests?

"I said to my wife, 'Look, she's a nice girl—our boy is happy—that's all that counts.' But we were worried about what our relatives would think.

"Well, we had a very nice wedding. The two brothers and a couple of cousins sang folk songs. Everybody danced. Everybody toasted the bride and groom. We had a fine time. And for days afterward, people kept calling to compliment us."

The basic points to keep in mind are the question, "Whose wedding is it?" and the answer, "It is my *child's* wedding." The most important people at the wedding are the bride and groom. Try to incorporate their wishes with yours, along with those of the other set of parents. This may not always be easy, but the results are worth the effort. Tell yourself that giving up part of *your* personal dream of the wedding can be your gift to your child. Your dream now—and its realization—can be the satisfaction of knowing that the couple will have a wonderful memory of *their* wedding to carry into the future.

Facing Underlying Problems

There are problems that may be worrisome, not only about the wedding, but about the marriage. Today, many young people have a mobility unheard of years ago. With increasing frequency, they are meeting—and marrying—people of backgrounds different from their own.

Economic Differences

- Is the other family noticeably richer or poorer than yours?
- How does this make you feel? Resentful, jealous, nervous, overanxious to please?
- Do you find yourself saying things not natural to you?

When great economic disparity is present between the two families, everyone may feel awkward. Acknowledging these feelings to yourself and your own family, and then addressing them in an honest and gentle way can help to bridge the gap.

Megan told us that before she met her future son-in-law's parents she was uneasy about the fact that they were very wealthy.

"My husband and I had talked to our daughter about the kind of wedding we could afford," said Megan, "and she was happy with our plans. Still, when the time came to meet the parents—they had invited us to Sunday dinner—I was afraid we would feel uncomfortable. Our daughter had told us that their house was exquisite, very grand.

"The house was very imposing but, fortunately, the parents were friendly and down-to-earth and fell right in with our plans. They told us they were going to give a party for the kids after the honeymoon. That was fine with us."

If uncomfortable feelings caused by economic or cultural differences do not fade away as easily as Megan's did, try to minimize the differences and concentrate on the similarities. Your child's future in-laws are parents, too. They, too, want their children to be happy. Work toward the goal of promoting harmony and ease between the families. And remember that many "problems" exist *mainly in our own minds.*

Geographic Distance

- Does one family live in Arizona and the other in Maine?
- Does the bride-to-be live a thousand miles away from her family—and the location of the wedding?
- How does one arrange a "long-distance" wedding?

Sometimes the physical distance is so great that neither family meets until just before the wedding.

In today's shrinking world, with quick communication and transportation, physical distance can be more of a challenge than a hardship. Yes, it does take time and effort to call or write, reporting on plans as they're being set or changed. It also involves trusting in the goodwill and good judgment of the host family, the other family, and the young people.

If the new couple is going to move to another part of the country following the wedding, you may be adding sadness to your other concerns. This sadness may be combined with resentment if the new location is the same as that of the other parents.

You may help yourself by establishing some particular routines or customs that will keep up a level of contact with your child, contact that will span the miles. A number of parents told us that they intersperse their telephone calls with short letters. One father sends notes on his "from the desk of" stationery from his office. Whenever he thinks of something to say, he jots it down and sends it off. Some parents have a schedule for calling, others use the spur of the moment method. The important thing here is not the method, but the communication itself. Check that not too much time elapses between contacts.

Cultural or Religious Differences

- Are you opposed to the marriage?
- Are the other parents opposed? Are you upset by their opposition, and resentful that they do not wholeheartedly welcome your child?
- Is there an issue of conversion? If so, and if it's a conversion *away* from your religion, how do you feel about it?

Solutions to these problems are never black and white. There is no right way or wrong way about what kind of wedding to have, or which marriage partner to choose. Again, a positive attitude, kindness, and respect for other patterns of living are the important factors in the future compatiblity of the families involved. A determination to be pleased, a wish to consider the other person's viewpoint, and, above all, a desire to see your child happy with the marriage partner of his or her choice may very well help to lessen your anxieties.

Sort out those aspects of the marriage that distress you. Discuss them with your child and your child's future spouse. Be candid in explaining just what worries you:

The interaction between two families of different religious or cultural backgrounds

The actual wedding proceedings—the ceremony, the place of the wedding, different wedding customs for the reception

And—perhaps your most important concern—the question of how the grandchildren will be raised

You may find it helpful to discuss your concerns with those dearest to you—family members, close friends, or a counselor or religious leader.

After reviewing all the aspects of the marriage:

- Think of as many favorable points as you can.
- Focus on the positive characteristics of your future in-law child.
- Work on your willingness to establish a good relationship with the couple.
- Be willing to have the bridal couple take the lead.

You have told your children how you feel. You have listened to the way they feel. Now it's time to let go of your strong position and to trust that your children will make a good life for themselves. This may mean compromises on your part. Be willing to accept these compromises.

Think about ways to calm yourself and put yourself at ease. Someone—often a person who is not on very familiar terms with you—may broach the subject of your child's marriage. If you're truly accepting in your own mind, you will convey a sense of ease to others.

If cultural and religious differences are not acknowledged and discussed early, they can fester and harden into scars so severe that it may seem as if they can never be removed. Stuart told us how he regretted his behavior toward his son's wife.

"I talked to my son till I was blue in the face," said Stuart. "At first, I refused to meet the girl, but both my wife and my son insisted on inviting her to dinner. I was rude to her—I couldn't help myself. I antagonized her right away. And you know what I did? I boycotted the wedding. My wife went, and my sister, and some of our friends, but I stayed away.

"If I had it to do over, I'd do it differently. My daughter-in-law has never forgiven me. We barely speak, even though I now have two grandchildren."

Laura's was a happier story. No less opposed to her child's marriage than Stuart was, she acted differently and got different results.

"I let my daughter know about my feelings right from the start," Laura told us. "We had never had intermarriage in the family before and I cringed at the very thought. I talked to my future son-in-law, too, describing the problems they both would face.

"He's a sweet fellow. He told me he understood my feelings, that his parents felt the same way, and that we should meet them.

"It's all worked out. We don't always agree, but we do respect each other."

You may not be able to erase lost years of coolness or alienation, nor can you obliterate differences between very disparate families. You can, however, blur some of those differences. You can use time, patience, and loving intentions to heal old wounds. Stuart's story can still have a happy ending. He need not spend the rest of his days living with the strain of being the "odd man out" in his family. It's not too late for him to say, "Sorry about the past—can we be friends?" Think of what he would be gaining!

Divorced Parents

If you or the other parents are divorced, or if your child or your child's prospective spouse has been married before and there are children from the previous marriage, you will need to keep these relationships in mind when you plan the wording of the invitations, the procession down the aisle, the seating arrangements, and other physical details of the wedding.

Divorce can produce problems beyond those involving protocol. Emotions are involved and, often, old wounds are reopened.

- How can the painful feelings caused by divorce be lessened, or at least put aside, at the wedding?
- How would your child feel if you or your former spouse:
    Stayed away from the wedding?
    Created an unpleasant scene?
    Acted with embarrassing coldness?
- How would your child feel about you and your role in such behavior?
- How could such behavior affect your future relationship with your child?

If your divorce was a bitter one, you may be in a quandary as to how to act at the wedding when you see your former spouse. Ask yourself how it would affect your child if you or your former spouse behaved badly at the wedding.

Joyce recalled the trepidation she experienced before her daughter's wedding.

"The wedding was to be the first time I was going to meet my ex-husband since the divorce," said Joyce. "Vic and I had parted so bitterly that I dreaded seeing him. He had sent my daughter a check for the wedding expenses, and I was taking care of all the arrangements.

"The day of the wedding, all I could think of was how I would handle seeing Vic. I decided to confront him—and my fear—all at once. I walked right over to him and said, 'Well, Vic, I want to congratulate you on our daughter's marriage.'

"It was the most amazing thing. His face had been as hard as stone, and then, suddenly, it relaxed. He actually smiled. 'I think they're going to have a happy life,' he said.

"That day at least," Joyce told us, "all of us had a wonderful time."

You cannot always bring about *perfect* circumstances, but by keeping the welfare of your child uppermost in your mind, you can often prevent old grievances from ruining the happiness of the occasion.

Finances

- Who pays for what?
- Who decides?

When Diane was planning her daughter's wedding, she and her husband decided on a small guest list and a modest reception. Her future son-in-law's family had other ideas.

"They wanted over a hundred people—just from their side," Diane said. "And they wanted a showy hotel with all the trimmings. They offered to pay more than half the cost.

"At first, we were tempted. It seemed the practical thing to do. But soon we realized we wanted our own kind of wedding.

"So, we talked with our daughter and our future son-in-law and found that they felt comfortable with our plans. Then we all talked to Jeremy's parents.

"They were disappointed, no doubt about it, and a little cool for a while, but it turned out all right. The wedding was lovely. And our new 'in-laws' seemed to enjoy the day as much as we did."

Financial considerations can vary among families. Consult etiquette books to get an idea of the "rules." Consult the young couple, and then the other parents.

Many circumstances can influence the financial arrangements: The bride has no family, or her family is very small, or very poor, or willing for the groom's family to pay for all or part of the wedding. Sharing expenses can be a practical idea, so long as both sides agree. Diane was offered financial assistance in making a large wedding. She declined the offer. She could just as correctly have elected to accept it.

If the groom's parents want a bigger or otherwise different wedding from the one being planned, they may wish to give a post-wedding reception for their friends and relatives.

The Guest List

- How many guests will be invited?
- Whose guests will they be?
- Who decides?

For many parents, whether the bride's or the groom's, the composition of the guest list—involved as it is with emotional and financial considerations—is fraught with anxiety and questions. Think about some possible answers.

If you are the maker of the party:

- Keep in mind a fair and cordial sharing of the guest list with the other family.
- Decide how much you are willing to compromise.
- Communicate with the other family.
- Show a willingness to compromise on certain issues.
- Try to foresee the consequences of an unpopular decision.
- Maintain your dignity—whatever your decision—and express respect for the others involved. Balance your "sense of self" with consideration for others.

If you are not the provider of the feast:

- Make up your list with consideration for your hosts. Keep in mind the parameters that have been set.
- Think about the guests you are choosing. Don't just invite people for the sake of inviting *someone*.

Whether you are the parent of the bride or of the groom:

- Select your guests with care. Think about how much *you* want them to attend the wedding, and how much you think *they* wish to attend.
- Keep in mind (when the list is being made) that it is the young people's wedding.
- Go over your list with them.
- Don't fall into the trap of saying, "I'll invite so-and-so. Surely they won't come." Be prepared for everyone on your list to attend, or you might end up with more people than you can handle.
- Be in charge of your list. Contact any people who do not respond on time to the invitation.

A wedding heralds a new era, not only for your child, but for you. The marriage of a child marks the completion of one kind of relationship and the beginning of another. Your child is now part of a pair, a couple. It can be a glorious time for all of you. Do your part in making it so.

Exercises

1. Write a "press release"—a newspaper announcement—of your child's wedding.
    - Ignore the space requirements of the newspaper. Make the announcement as long as you wish.

- Describe *your* version of a dream wedding for your child.
- Include all the details you can think of:
    Occupation and education of the young couple
    Occupation and education of the parents
    Bride's wedding gown
    Family background, famous or prominent relatives
    Place of the ceremony
    Who officiated
    Place of the reception
    Number of guests

2. Read the press release, and then reread it.
   - Consciously examine the order, emphasis, and amount of space you gave to the various details.
   - Write down what you emphasized.
   - Write down what you think you slid over or perhaps omitted entirely.

3. Analyze the press release.
   - Does it tell you anything about your opinions and desires for the wedding?
   - Do you think the physical order of the items shows their order of importance to you?
   - How important is each item to you?
   - Is there any significance in the details you may have omitted?
   - How many of the details that are important to you are within the realm of possibility? How many are financially feasible?

4. Write another press release, this time from the standpoint of your child's wishes.
   - Try to put yourself in your child's mind. List all the details that you think your child wants for the wedding.

5. Compare the two releases.

- Do they differ sharply in the main details (one list placed the wedding in your living room, the second in a catering hall)?
- Are you willing to change some parts of your dream in favor of your child?
- How do you feel about the changes?

6. Show both press releases to your child—or to the young couple. Discussing the details may help to clear the air of differences or disagreements.

7. As you do additional drafts of the release, does it get closer to your child's dream?

Chapter 7

Married Children: Changes in the Family Tree

So much has been said about the adjustment young couples have to make when they marry that sometimes we lose sight of the adjustment that has to be made by their parents. Because many adult children lead independent lives for several years before they marry, their parents have already made the adjustment to their children's physical absence. Often an emotional adjustment still has to be made.

The marriage of a child is one of life's milestones, regarded by many parents as both an official separation and a new beginning. The child may have been a mature adult for a number of years, with a career, an apartment, and a private life, but the parents had a one-to-one relationship with that child. Suddenly, a stranger appears on the scene, a person parents are "supposed to" welcome into their family, a partner for their child, a rival for their love. These simultaneous emotions of separation and a new beginning can also affect the adult children. Torn between loyalty to their parents and loyalty to the new spouse—and the new spouse's family—they can feel confused, guilty, and pulled apart.

Be of good cheer. The picture is not as bleak as it might seem. As a parent, you may undergo a period of adjustment, but this adjustment does not have to be either severe or prolonged.

If you have any negative feelings, don't try to ignore or stifle them; don't try to change them all at once. Think about these feelings, pull them out of their dark hiding places, and expose them to the light. Confront them. Mull them over in your mind. You may wish to write them down.

Identify Negative Feelings

The distress that some parents experience covers a wide spectrum. What may trouble one family may never be noticed by another. Some of these feelings are conscious, others less so; many are barely acknowledged. What follows is a list culled from the many comments we have heard. You may consider some to be serious, others frivolous and barely worth mentioning. Every family has a different way of thinking and a different way of acting. Listening to other people's objections can help you to think about your own, to confront them, to give them new perspective, and to cause them to lose some of their anxiety-producing power.

You can then ask yourself:

- What happens next?
- How can I focus my attention on mitigating, changing, or letting go of these feelings?
- How can I strengthen the relationship with my child?
- How can I build a healthy relationship with my child's spouse?

"I Can't Believe My Baby Is Married"

Some parents find it difficult to adjust to the basic idea of their children's marriage, and so they look for reasons to justify their unease.

The feelings related by one parent may seem extreme, but several parents expressed similar sentiments.

"When my son married," said Jerry, "I was in shock. I said to myself, 'This is it—the family is finished—we won't be close anymore—I'll never be able to talk to him again the way I used to.'

"I liked my daughter-in-law, but I kept thinking that she took him away from me. Every time I saw the two of them together, I thought of my son as having a divided loyalty. I felt he no longer belonged to us. He didn't care about us anymore.

"And I blamed her."

When Jerry said, "I felt he no longer belonged to us," he seemed unaware that children do not *belong* to parents. Parents raise their children, love them, and strive for a special relationship with them. But parents do not "own" their children, and children do not "belong" to their parents.

Jerry eventually adjusted to his son's marriage. He had never actually quarreled with his daughter-in-law, had never been critical or unkind. He had maintained a distance from her that was beginning to extend to his son.

"It got so that my son and I barely talked about anything more significant than the weather," said Jerry.

"I didn't know what to do. I discussed the matter with some friends who advised me to be truthful with my son.

"My son and I met for lunch, and I immediately told him that things were different between us, that I felt we had lost a lot of what we used to have together, and that I felt bad about it. I never mentioned my daughter-in-law. I put everything on myself.

"We talked for over two hours. My son told me he, too, felt miserable. He said he'd been feeling 'torn.' "

After they talked, father and son embraced. Jerry told us that from that day, he has felt . . .

". . . comfortable and *safe*. My son and I are much closer now. And I talk to my daughter-in-law—small talk, mostly, but friendly. I feel relieved. I think we all do."

To some parents, the word *loyalty* has a flip side: *dis*loyalty. Their child's attention to the new spouse seems to be equated with disloyalty toward *them*. Other parents may feel a sense of separation, even of loss. Many parents speak of family customs that are no longer the same—of how the married daughter missed the Fourth of July picnic last year, and the married son missed the annual Cousins' Club reunion.

It is not only at holiday time that you may experience a sense of loss. A new family unit has been formed, one that is distinct and separate from yours. Perhaps, remembering your own early married life, you are casting a wistful eye or—subconsciously— a jealous one on the new family. Perhaps you fear that your own family unit is now diminished.

As in so many aspects of our lives, our attitudes can determine how we cope with various situations, and what we make of them. Your family unit will be diminished only if you allow it to be.

- Acknowledge your feelings to yourself—loss, separation, awkwardness, sadness.
- Feel the pain; allow yourself to grieve.
- Talk about it with other family members or friends.
- Allow yourself to let go of these sad feelings; allow the sadness to dissolve.
- Move on to other things; do something that will make you happy.

Your child understandably is loyal to the new spouse. This need not diminish the love and caring felt for you. Instead of thinking in terms of divided loyalties, think in terms of sharing. Create new customs, new times for fun. The Fourth of July picnic need not be the only high point of the summer. If practical, seize opportunities for unplanned, last-minute activities. They can be the most fun of all.

"I'm Not Comfortable With My Child's Spouse"

Various factors may be at work here. Parents may feel threatened; they may see themselves as losing influence or status. They may look upon the in-law child as the symbol of the changes taking place in their own lives.

The relationship between your in-law child and his or her own parents may give you some insight. That relationship may be overly close, unstable, or even estranged. You may be receiving some of the backlash.

If the in-law child comes from a different ethnic, religious, or socioeconomic background, you may feel awkward or resentful.

Sheila remembered how upset she was when her daughter married a young man of a different religion.

"I tried to talk them out of it, told them about all the obstacles ahead, but they wouldn't listen.

"After the wedding, I couldn't face anyone. I refused to see my friends. I was actually making myself ill.

"Then, my husband and I sat down and talked, and we figured out that the main thing that bothered me was what people were thinking about my daughter's marriage—what they were thinking, and what they were saying. It made me deal with my own carefully hidden prejudices.

"I was then able to see my son-in-law as he is—a fine young man who loves my daughter. I feel better now about the marriage."

Another source of discomfort can occur if your son-in-law or daughter-in-law has been married before and has a child from that marriage.

"This is not what I wanted for my son," Alan told us. "I don't like the idea of him being saddled with another man's child. What does that make me—a step-grandfather?"

Alan's words, "what I wanted for my son," are akin to Jerry's statement, "he no longer belonged to us." We may want certain things for our children, good things—a fulfilling career, a happy marriage. But, we do not own our children. What we want for them may not be what they want for themselves. It's the right of all adults to determine the shape and direction of their own lives.

Your child's spouse is not your child. You did not raise the in-law child; he or she may have traits, values, and ideas that are different from yours. Go slowly. A smile, a compliment, a sympathetic nod all help to make a rough road smooth.

When there are differences, respect them. Be understanding and willing to learn. Your whole outlook, indeed, your whole life, may be broadened.

"My daughter married a Russian," Marian told us, "a citizen of Moscow. He came to the United States six years ago, as a member of a skating team. My daughter was in public relations, and that's how they met.

"We were frightened and suspicious at first, my husband and I. Was this young man renouncing his country and his family to marry an American—any American—in order to become a citizen?

"We went along with their plans—my daughter seemed so happy. But everything about him was strange. He hardly spoke to us, and, when he did speak, his eyes kept shifting from side to side. We wondered if this was a national trait—or if he was either looking for spies or waiting to be arrested.

"Ah, poor boy, we've since learned that he was much more frightened than we. He's a wonderful person, and has become like a son to us. He has shared stories about his Russian background with us—everything from old family tales to his grandmother's wonderful recipes. Not long ago, we went to Russia and met his family.

"It was a lucky day when my daughter met him. We've all turned out to be winners."

"We've all turned out to be winners." Marian and her family changed what they originally perceived as potentially negative circumstances into a warm, rich relationship. It turned out that her son-in-law truly was worthy of their trust. Marian's willingness to broaden her experiences certainly helped ease things along.

Sometimes parents may be so enthusiastic about the child's coming marriage that they can overwhelm the young couple. Be wary of becoming too familiar all at once. A little reserve in the beginning, mixed with lots of respect, can grow into a close and stable relationship.

If your in-law child has been married before, there may be various complications. A child from that marriage, plus the appearances of the ex-spouse in connection with the child, can cause strain on your adult child, your in-law child, and the rest of the family. Do your part to ease the situation by not volunteering opinions or taking sides. Be helpful, friendly, and not judgmental.

When Alan spoke of his son being "saddled with another man's child," he made his position clear. He was dissatisfied with the situation. It is to be hoped that Alan kept his thoughts to himself, although, as we all know, it is very difficult to keep our feelings from showing.

Another parent may react differently and may be delighted at becoming an "instant grandparent."

"My Child Has Changed: He Acts Differently Toward Me"

Negative reactions may result if parents feel that the adult child is now treating them differently—perhaps on a more "equal" level. The parents may not want to be "equal"; they may want to continue their traditional role.

Or they may see their child as condescending, even rude. They may go so far as blaming the in-law child for their son's or daughter's new behavior—as Jerry did. These parents may not yet have faced the fact that their child is adult and mature, and *separate* from them. A newly married child may be uncertain in the new role and perhaps may overreact. Be patient.

Again, attitude plays a big part. A parent can rejoice in this new "equal" relationship and can feel more like a "friend." Of course, the relationship between parent and child is never exactly equal, nor are parent and child ever exactly friends in the same way as age-peers. These words and their definitions are unimportant. What matters is the relationship itself—a warm, loving, caring, *special* interaction between adults.

"My Child Married Too Young"

This may simply reflect parents' unwillingness to accept their children's adult status. Or, they may be unwilling to admit that they are old enough to have a married child. It can also be a subconscious way for parents to put into concrete terms their uneasiness with or distaste for the marriage itself. After all, "too young" is ambiguous. *And*, considering that the child is already married, what can be gained from such an objection? One woman said that, although *she* married at twenty, "things are not the same as they were. Twenty today is different from the way it was when I married. Adolescence lasts longer now. Kids don't have the seriousness they used to; they don't assume responsibilities anymore."

Such rationalizations can be harmful. They can color your thinking and influence your actions. Refrain from nit-picking and looking for excuses to find fault with the marriage. Such behavior can put unnecessary stress on your child's marriage.

"Right After the Wedding, the Kids Moved Across the Country"

"How can I feel close to them when we're in Boston and they're in Seattle?" Variations of this cry are heard over and over. Our country is huge, our society mobile. If the young couple moves far away, the parent can feel abandoned or rejected.

Effective long-distance parenting involves a positive attitude and some creative planning.

It's easy and understandable to complain about the distance, easy to feel hurt or disappointed that the children moved so far away. It's more constructive to recognize the reason for the move. Some adult children may move away to satisfy a desire for adventure, or to gain independence and put a little "space" between them and their childhood ties. This need not reflect on you or your child-raising skills. Often, the young husband or wife is offered a job or career opportunity too good to turn down.

The phenomenon of young people moving away is not new. Our country was founded by pioneers—immigrants who left their parents and families and came to explore the new world. Many of their descendants then uprooted themselves and set out for the west.

Your attitude can do much to ease the situation and reduce feelings of resentment or guilt.

- Talk to your children about the move.
- Tell them how you feel about it—that you are sad they will be living so many miles away.

- Avoid making your children feel guilty.
- Express enthusiasm about their career goals.
- As opportunities and circumstances permit, plan visits back and forth.

Long-distance parenting requires a combination of imagination and realism. To prevent the physical distance from limiting the relationship, it is important to keep in touch by visiting, writing letters, and making telephone calls.

Sidney's wife lamented, "I feel abandoned and rejected since the children moved away." Sidney thought about how he might comfort her. He called the airlines and immediately scheduled periodic visits to the children.

He also subscribed to a telephone system that reduced long-distance rates, so that he and his wife would not hesitate to call frequently.

Visiting

We all know that airports and train stations are jammed at Thanksgiving and Christmas. What about scheduling a visit for February or August or September? There are plenty of bargains during off-peak months if you can take advantage of them.

Before visiting, do some research on the area, perhaps planning some side trips. You will increase your pleasure during the trip and your children's pride in their new location. In addition, if the visit is for more than a few days, you will free your children from having to take you sightseeing, reduce any burden on them, and not feel like an intruder.

While visiting, refrain from saying things like, "What's so great about this place? What have you got here that you didn't have at home?"

Letter-writing

Whatever happened to letters; does anyone write them anymore? Forget the "How are you, I'm fine" variety; ditto, the long soul-searchers. Keep paper handy and jot down a sentence from time to time. Nothing fancy, no deep probings, and no "Why haven't you written until now?" Just random thoughts, descriptions of social occasions, news of the family and the neighborhood. Good to tuck into your envelopes are magazine and newspaper articles, book reviews, bits of trivia—anything that might interest your adult child. Photographs add a personal touch. Some parents and their children mail audio or video tapes. One parent told us that her children sent her a fax of the sonogram of her future grandchild. "Amazing," she said. "How's that for using the latest technology! I felt so good, as if the kids lived next door."

Telephone Calls

Phone calls can be a pleasure or a chore. If the calls are not to become the old familiar "weather reports"—how are you, how is your job, how are the children, and, of course, how is the weather out there—plan some subjects in advance, using the same sort of topics you use for letters. Figure out the good times for calling—when it's comfortable and convenient and not intrusive for you or your child. Make your calls on a spontaneous basis if that is practical. Make them fairly short and breezy—or make them long if that's the mood of the day.

The telephone answering machine, often denounced as a modern nuisance, can be a blessing when an adult child lives far away. Some parents said that being able to leave a message makes them feel good.

"It sure beats sitting there listening to the endless drone of the rings at the other end," said one father. "My wife and I try to jazz up our messages. We'll tell a joke or a quick story. And then, a day or two later, if we've not been home, we'll find a similar type of message from our son on our machine."

Other parents also liked the answering machine. One parent mentioned that when she came home from vacation recently . . .

". . . I turned on the machine and heard my daughter's voice: 'I know you won't be home until later, but I have to leave now. I just wanted to say hello.'

"I loved it! I considered it a 'welcome home' call."

Frequent communication keeps the relationship alive. Shared thoughts, written and spoken, help to nourish the relationship, whether parent and child live a few hours away from each other or at opposite ends of the country. Events occur in your and your children's lives—simple, nonearthshaking events, such as reading an interesting book, seeing a good film, buying a piece of furniture, meeting an old friend. If you cover only "important" topics in your letters and calls, and if you allow too much time to elapse between contacts, you and your children can lose a sense of involvement with each other. But aim for moderation. Don't force the contacts. There are times when you and your child may need a little less involvement with each other, when you need a little of the "space" we mentioned before. Use your judgment.

Letters and telephone calls are not a substitute for personal contact, but life is not perfect—whoever said it was? The old proverb, "Absence makes the heart grow fonder," is nonsense. Absence makes the heart forget; letters and phone calls help the heart remember.

"I Can't Get Used to a Strange Fellow Calling Me 'Dad' "

Some parents have trouble with "titles." Should the in-law child address them as Mom and Dad? Many people prefer the new spouse to call them by their first names. Some families use

Mr. and Mrs.—although in our present-day rather casual society, others might find this a bit stiff and formal.

Howard told us how he and his wife handled this situation.

"We saw that our daughter-in-law stammered whenever she addressed us as Mom and Dad," said Howard. "So we asked her what would make her comfortable. She said she would prefer calling us by our first names. It's worked out fine. We all speak to each other with respect and affection. That's what's important!"

If you're not comfortable with the title your in-law child is now using, discuss it. State your preference. If it does not match his or hers, aim for a compromise. If the result is not entirely satisfactory, let a quote from Shakespeare give you some cheer: "What's in a name? A rose by any other name would smell as sweet."

"I Don't Care for My Daughter-in-law's Family"

Interacting with your child's in-laws may take a little time. You may have gotten to know them during your child's engagement, or you may have met them just before the wedding. Perhaps their way of life seems strange to you; perhaps their opinions and ideas are at odds with yours. But, no matter how great the differences between the two families, both have one important thing in common—the young couple.

Knowing that your child spends time with the new in-laws, and hearing your child call them "Mom" and "Dad," may make you feel uncomfortable, but after a while you will get used to it. Do what you can to ensure respect between the two families.

What if the other family is not treating your child in a loving or respectful way? What if your child complains about them to you?

The first thing you can do is listen. Then, gently and discreetly, react to the story you are told. While avoiding the use of critical, demeaning adjectives about the in-law family, express your love of, support for, and confidence in your child. Without giving advice, you can ask your child to think first about the changes he or she would like in the relationship, and then how to bring about these changes.

Mary Ellen's daughter, Stacy, was having difficulty getting along with her mother-in-law. Mary Ellen suggested to her daughter that they engage in some role playing, a technique she had learned at an awareness group she attended.

> "First," said Mary Ellen, "Stacy played herself and I played her mother-in-law. I started to criticize her, told her that her hair was too long, that she should wear more makeup, that she didn't feed my 'son' enough proper food. Stacy acted the way she always did with her real mother-in-law—she was unresponsive and sullen.
>
> "Then we reversed the roles. Stacy gave her 'daughter-in-law' the same kind of criticism. I was now playing Stacy, and this is the way I responded: 'Mother, aren't you glad to have me visit? I really feel hurt and angry each time I come. I feel inadequate. I feel that I can't do anything right.' "

In this way, the daughter-in-law refrained from actually criticizing her mother-in-law's behavior. She spoke in the first person: *I* feel hurt and angry; *I* feel inadequate. She took responsibility for the way she felt.

It is to be hoped that the mother-in-law would respond in an understanding way, and that the situation would improve. At any rate, the daughter-in-law was now able to unbottle her feelings and perhaps would interact better with her mother-in-law in the future.

Doing your part in fostering a good relationship between the two families is a great gift to give to the young couple.

- Avoid making your child feel guilty about spending time with the in-law family.

- Avoid criticizing or gossiping about the in-law family, either to the in-law child or your own child.
- Avoid fostering tension between your child and the in-law family.
- Avoid any semblance of interfering.
- Encourage your child to be warm and friendly to the new family.
- Include the new family in some of your own family plans.

Emphasize Positive Feelings: Strengthen the Relationship

Recognize, accept, and acknowledge your child's independence. Your child is now part of a couple, a team. What is the basic ingredient of a successful team? Team spirit! By respecting the team and by demonstrating your goodwill, you will foster this spirit and help the new couple off on a positive path.

Continue being a loving and caring parent. Let go, but do not disconnect! Show your love, but—and it is a big but—bear in mind that in your anxiety to make everything safe and good for each member of the family, you can, however unintentionally, regress into the role of trying to be in command. Sometimes, unwittingly, you may make a suggestion that is perceived by the child as a directive.

Brian kept "putting his foot in his mouth" by saying whatever occurred to him. His daughter, who had a "very short fuse," kept accusing him of being bossy. Brian had to defend himself, make excuses, and deny being bossy.

"I decided to be frank," said Brian. " 'Look, you two,' I told my daughter and son-in-law, 'maybe I did sound as if I was questioning your judgment. All I wanted was to make sure you thought about it a little more before you signed that lease.'

"We had a good talk, about a lot of different things. We really cleared the air. They're not so touchy anymore, and I'm a little more sensitive to their feelings."

Do not berate yourself, or even be over-cautious. Be sensitive and aware of your child's reaction, and ready to back off or talk it out.

Married people have disagreements. They may argue or bicker. If you overhear your child arguing with his or her spouse, turn a deaf ear. If you are in the room, walk out. If you are elsewhere in the house—out of sight, but within earshot—feign ignorance. If, separately or together, they should want to discuss their quarrel with you, tread very carefully. Listen quietly and sympathetically. Be soothing and reassuring, but noncommittal. Above all, *don't take sides.*

If they continue to air their grievances, you might wish to ask a question, such as, "Jason, how would you like things to be between you and Tina?" or, "Tina, what would you like from Jason?" The adult child or the adult couple may not be seeking actual advice; they may merely want the reassurance of knowing that someone else is listening.

Listening to your child in an understanding way helps to strengthen the bond between you. It creates a climate of trust and support and removes any hint of your being "a know-it-all."

One parent had to restrain herself from being "too helpful."

"I've had to teach myself to hold back a little. When my daughter comes to me with a problem, it doesn't always mean that she wants me to provide a solution. In the past I was always ready to give an instant answer.

"Recently my daughter told me, 'Mom, I don't need to have you solve my problem. I just need to have you listen to me.' "

To keep caring, without seeming to take charge, is easier to say than to do. When you are worried about how your children are leading their daily lives, it may be comfortable—and tempting—to give advice. Resist the temptation.

- Be patient with yourself, and with your children.
- Allow time for the in-law relationship to develop. It does not have to be "instant love."
- Respect your child's new loyalties.
- Consider your in-law child as, if not yet a member of the family, then a potentially dear friend.
- Look upon the marriage as an opportunity:
  to expand the family.
  to meet new people.
  to have many occasions for joyous celebrations.

Many parents have the good fortune to enjoy a new rapport with their children when their children marry. They have more in common now and find the relationship better than ever. Moreover, many parents achieve a special closeness with their in-law children, a supportive, impartial kind of closeness that manifests itself during times of stress—and during good times, too!

Reflections

1. Recall your in-laws' first visit to your home.
   - Did you feel comfortable with your in-laws as your guests?
   - If not, why were you uncomfortable?
   - Did you feel inadequate as a host?
   - Did you feel reduced to "little child" status?
   - Did you feel out of control in your own home?
2. Now, picture yourself visiting your recently married children.
   - How can you put them at ease?
   - What do you think they would like to hear from you?
     Acknowledgment?
     Compliments?
   - Can you picture yourself treating the young couple:
     With respect?
     With sensitivity?
     With love?

Exercises

1. Questions to ask yourself:
   - Do you disapprove of your adult children's choices?
   - Do you express this disapproval to them?
   - Do you try to be supportive of them?
   - Do you find yourself taking sides in your children's disagreements with each other?
   - Do you criticize your in-law child to your own child?
   - Do you criticize your child to your in-law child?
   - Do you openly share with your children your experiences as a young married person in a friendly and non-judgmental way, so that they may adopt whatever they find useful?
2. Repeat these questions one at a time.
   - Answer each question as honestly as you can.
   - Think about the various situations or circumstances that might have led to your behavior.
   - If you wish to alter your behavior, or the situations or circumstances that have led to it, think about how you can do so.

Chapter 8

Grandparenting: A Second Chance?

Becoming a grandparent has been described in various rhapsodic terms, ranging from reliving one's youth, to having all the joys of raising a child without having the day-to-day responsibilities. One parent described this stage in her life as giving her a surprising dividend.

> "I expected to love that baby," said Betty, "and boy, do I ever! What I didn't expect was the utter happiness I've gotten from watching my son become such a wonderful father.
>
> "And there's an added thrill. My son sings the same songs and plays the same games he learned from us. The continuity of life keeps unfolding before my eyes. It's a miracle."

Another parent felt he was given a "second chance."

> "When my kids were little," said William, "I wasn't what you'd call an active father. I loved my kids, but I didn't get down and roll on the floor with them. I certainly didn't participate in the physical side of their upbringing.

I was busy with my job, and anyway, the nitty-gritty side of raising kids was considered 'woman's work.'

"Well, it's a different world now, and I feel part of it. I give my grandchild her bottle, I feed her, I give her a bath. I'm having the time of my life."

Old Stereotypes: Forget Them

For many of us, grandparenting is coming later in life than it did for our parents. As a result, we have had the time to engage in activities that are not family-related—careers, volunteer work, travel, hobbies.

If we picture the old storybook images of how grandparents looked and acted, we probably will find them quite different from the way we picture ourselves. Maybe this is an exaggeration, maybe not. But, although we may not all see ourselves in the old stereotypes, and although modern grandparents may look different or act differently from grandparents of a few generations back, most of us wholeheartedly enjoy being with our grandchildren.

Your New Role: Define It for Yourself

Joyful, successful grandparenting requires a little thought and planning. Set the tone for close, happy family ties. Have fun with your grandchildren, always remembering that it is your *child* who is now the parent. The love you show your grandchildren has to be grounded in support for the new parent. Find your own ways of showing that love. Integrate the role of grandparent into the other parts of your life, keeping respect for your own wishes and your own standards.

Whether you are already a grandparent or are about to become one, think about the kind of grandparent you wish to be. How available are you? How available do you want to be?

Sometimes the young parents have a picture of the way their

own grandparents involved themselves in family life and are disappointed when we do not conform to their old image.

Think about the various roles that a grandparent could have: nursemaid, adviser, support person, party and good times person, spur-of-the-moment person at any time, spur-of-the-moment person only in times of crisis. Many grandparents want to travel a middle road. They want to be helpful and involved—but only up to a point. It is up to you to pick that point.

- Choose your own standards of grandparenting.
- Choose the kind and amount of involvement that you want.
- Choose the kind of relationship that you want.

These decisions are not always easy. Charlotte said that she often felt "pulled in all directions."

"I had established an active life for myself," said Charlotte, "but since my grandchild was born I'm afraid to make any advance plans. My daughter and her family live ten minutes away. It's great to have them so near, but it does cause some problems.

"My daughter has been having trouble getting a reliable baby-sitter. So, at about eight in the morning, I'll get a call—'Ma, the sitter isn't here. I'll be late for work. Could you come?'

"I love watching my grandchild, but not full-time. I feel like a doctor who's constantly on call."

Several parents related similar stories.

"My daughter is divorced," said James, "and my ex-son-in-law lives in another state. My grandchild needs a surrogate father, and I've been elected. I like taking my grandson to baseball games and museums. But I like doing it on my own initiative and not as part of a rigid weekend schedule.

"I haven't said anything yet to my daughter, but I'm beginning to sense a bit of a strain between us. I think we're both feeling guilty. But what can we do? My grandchild does need a male figure in his life."

Such situations, if prolonged, can cause you stress, as well as inconvenience. Both Charlotte and James need to have frank discussions with their children, expressing their love for their children and grandchildren, and their willingness—even eagerness—to be involved in their grandchildren's lives, but on a more spontaneous basis. Alternate choices can be made by the young parents.

The time and energy you give to your grandchildren does not have to be based on how your adult children conduct their lives. It should be based on the kind of involvement you want and how it fits into your life.

- Set your own priorities. Child care may be high on your list, or it may not.
- Talk with your child. Listen to your child's situation; describe your own.
- When you wish to be available, make that clear.
- When you wish to be unavailable, make that clear also.
- Put your own intentions first—but be conscious of special needs, emergencies, or other altering factors.
- Wait until asked to help—but pick up clues.

The decisions you make are not engraved in stone. You can, when you wish, change your decisions, compromise, make adjustments, and consider the needs of others. By being sympathetic and understanding, and by demonstrating that you have your own schedule and concerns, you will help your child to take responsibility for his or her own life.

A Grandparent: Not a Parent

Grandparenting sometimes serves as an excuse for *one-upmanship* of a parent over the adult child. First comes the implication that "I know all about raising children. I've done it, and that makes me an expert." From there, it is easy to progress to giving orders: "Never mind what the doctor says—start him on cereal now." It is then but a step to criticizing the young parent's competence: "I can't believe that you'd take a three-month-old baby to a restaurant."

The basic rule of being a loving, wise grandparent is to tell yourself that you are a *grand*parent—grand, meaning *great* and *wonderful*—not disapproving, scolding, or judging harshly, indeed, not judging at all. Examine your reactions. Child-rearing today is different from the way it used to be. It is more relaxed and casual. And even if it were not, does it really matter if the baby gets his cereal a month "late," or goes to a restaurant where he can get a little "social education" at a tender age? But, whether it matters or not, remember that you are the grandparent, not the parent. Give your love to your grandchild, and your love and support to your adult child.

Alice was excited by the prospect of a week-long visit with her son's family in Atlanta. She had not seen her grandchildren in six months and had never been able to spend a whole week with them. Her husband's retirement made new things possible in their lives—and this was one change she was looking forward to with glee. She hoped there would be many such trips.

The first day of the visit, Alice thought that her grandchildren looked taller than she remembered but, she noted, they were lean and wiry. "Are they too thin," she wondered, "or do they just take after Jeannine's family—they are all lithe and lissome."

On the second day of the visit Grandmother Alice started to pay closer attention to mealtimes and in-between snacks. By the third day, she felt herself becoming anxious and worried.

The children, who were two and five years old, stayed at the table only briefly at each mealtime. They talked, they played, they ate a mouthful or two of food, and left. Alice continued to worry. By the fourth day, she positioned herself between the children at the table. She tried to hold the younger one on her lap. He slithered off. She tried to play a game of "Here comes the airplane!" It worked once or twice, but that was all. Alice felt frustrated and upset.

Her daughter-in-law, Jeannine, waited until after dinner and then asked Alice to please stop displaying to the children her anxiety about food. Alice felt defensive. She protested that she was concerned about the children's weight and the fact that they ate so poorly.

Jeannine tried to reassure her that the children had regular physical checkups and were in good health. She explained that children's eating patterns change as they develop, and nagging them would be counterproductive.

Alice realized that she needed to accept the ideas and attitudes current for her children's generation. She let go of having to be right and trusted that her son and daughter-in-law were taking proper care of their children. For the rest of the visit, Alice practiced simply enjoying their company.

What do you do if you disagree with the way the young parents are handling an aspect of child care that you deem vital or serious? Some of your concerns might be:

Health:
Your grandchildren are always coming down with colds and infections. You believe that they are not being served enough nutritious food.

Safety:

One of your grandchildren is allowed to ride a bicycle, another to take driving lessons. You consider both children too young for such activities.

Values:

Your grandchildren are constantly given expensive toys by their parents. After a short time, the toys are broken or abandoned. You are concerned that your grandchildren are not being made aware of the value of money.

Social Graces:

Your grandchildren are not being taught the finer points of etiquette. You are worried that they are growing up rude and awkward.

Naturally, you want your grandchildren to grow up in a good environment. You want them healthy and happy. If you see an aspect of their upbringing that makes you uneasy, what do you do—talk to your children, talk to your grandchildren, talk openly, talk around the subject?

Think about the problem first. Decide how important it is, not to you, but to the welfare of your grandchild. Speak to the parent if you feel you must.

- Express your opinion once, and then back off.
- Speak calmly and rationally.
- Respect the parent's opinion.
- Be careful not to make your adult child feel like a "bad parent."

You can try an indirect approach:

- Share with your grandchild activities that reflect your interests and values.

    Take your grandchild to your workshop; make a toy, a shelf, some bookends.

Take your grandchild to stores, a museum, a restaurant.
Plan various projects for you to do together—gardening, cooking, sewing, participating in sports.
Read stories and poems aloud.

Gift Giving: Make It Your Choice

Most grandparents like to give their grandchildren gifts, but sometimes the giving can get out of hand. When pleasure turns into obligation, when you feel you have to "keep up" with the other grandparents, or when your adorable grandchild always greets you at the door with, "What did you bring me?" you know that things have gotten a little out of hand.

As a grandparent, you are the one to decide on the "what, when, and if" of gift giving without being influenced either by current fads or other people.

"Being on a merry-go-round," is the way Fran described her situation.

"The harder I try to get off," said Fran, "the faster the merry-go-round goes. My son's in-laws are lovely people, but they've gone completely insane over our mutual granddaughter. Our daughter-in-law is Elyse and Carl's only child, and Amanda is their first grandchild.

"We're crazy about Amanda, too, but we have three children and now we have five grandchildren. I love them all, am devoted to them, and love to spend time with them. But I have to divide my time—and my money.

"Elyse and Carl have been heaping presents on Amanda from the day she was born: dolls, books, games, puzzles—everything they can find.

"I've never thought of myself as competitive, but I get a little self-conscious when I come in with a plastic boat that costs a dollar, and they're carrying a huge doll that talks and cries.

"I feel as if I'm a TV sitcom caught in the ratings war. Which side is going to win?"

A gift to a small child does not have to be expensive or elaborate. We have all heard the story of the child who has every toy imaginable but who loves to play with an old coffeepot.

You can bring your grandchild crayons and colored construction paper. You can cut illustrations of birds and animals from magazines and bring them or mail them. Children love to receive their own mail, with their name and a real stamp on the envelope. You can bring cookies. You can bring the ingredients for cookies, so that you and your grandchild can have a baking session together. You can give part of yourself—child care in the very early years and companionship and friendship as the child grows older. And, sometimes, in answer to the question, "What did you bring me?" you can reply, "Today, sweetie, I brought myself. Choose one of your books—any book you like—and I'll read to you."

Another Set of Grandparents: Share the Joy

Various factors can determine the kind of relationship you have with the other grandparents—the similarities or differences in your backgrounds, your interests and lifestyles, and geographic proximity.

Unwittingly, like Fran, you may find yourself competing with them. A tug-of-war (overt or not immediately obvious) between the two sets of grandparents can encompass many areas. Which set of grandparents is more important in the life of the new baby, the young child, the growing teenager? Which set is more generous, more considerate, more considered? And, of course, which set brings better gifts?

The idea of "keeping up with the Joneses" has plagued people for years. Refuse to fall into that trap. Avoid getting locked into a competitive game—of gifts, child care, or anything else. Aim for spontaneity and self-determination. Build a unique relationship with your grandchild.

Another trap to avoid is the one in which you feel ignored and neglected. The other grandparents seem to be invited much more than you. You feel left out. You may feel frustrated or limited in your relationship with your grandchild because your in-law child does not give you equal opportunities for bonding as offered to the other grandparents.

Examine the circumstances and focus on the result you want. Is it that you want to spend more time with your grandchild? Then simply say that to your adult children. Be direct and clear. Avoid being accusatory or playing the victim. If, after your best efforts, the results are disappointing, you may have to accept the situation and work within it to enjoy the company of your grandchildren as much as possible.

"New Age" Experiences: How to Cope

Your Child Divorces

If your child is divorced and your in-law child takes the children a thousand miles away, as the grandparent, what do you do?

If you had a good relationship with your in-law child, the likelihood is that it will continue after the divorce—with the joint intention of having the grandparent-grandchild relationship continue. If the relationship was unsatisfactory, do your part to remain in touch. Be patient, and try to improve the relationship with letters and small gifts.

You may gain a feeling of comfort and support by talking this over with an adviser. You may find that support in the person of a counselor, friend, or lawyer.

Different Lifestyles

Leo had worked hard at accepting the fact that his daughter is gay and living with another woman, but he was saddened by the thought that he would never be a grandfather. He had another adjustment in store for him when his daughter announced that she was pregnant. She and her partner planned to raise the child together.

What were Leo's choices? He might have viewed this development as a big embarrassment; he might have decided to ignore the child. He chose instead to become a loving grandfather and support his daughter in her decision. "You have a wonderful baby," Leo told his daughter. "She looks just like you when you were that age. I love her."

In a parallel situation, John had never accepted his daughter's gay lifestyle. "If she wants to live this way," he said, "I can't stop her, but I don't have to condone it either."

When the baby was born, he stayed away. Two years later, at a family picnic, he saw the baby for the first time. He could not resist picking him up and embracing him. John was quickly caught up in the pleasures of being a grandfather.

You may not be prepared to sanction your child's unconventional lifestyle, but why deprive yourself and your grandchild of what could be a loving and rich relationship?

Second Time Around: Raising Your Grandchildren

> "I never dreamed that we'd be rearing small children again," said Sally. "But what else could we do? My son-in-law deserted his family when the second child was born, and my daughter is still under treatment for drug addiction.
>
> "Our grandchildren are very precious to us, but, boy, what a change they've made in our lives."

Sally and her husband are not unique. Many grandparents today find themselves, for various reasons, in the role of parent to their grandchildren. Many of them are able to do it willingly, even joyfully; others find it overwhelming, physically, emotionally, or financially. For some grandparents, it is impossible to take on this responsibility. Other arrangements must be made. The grandparents will have to deal with their sadness and make plans to maintain a relationship with the grandchildren.

Grandparents' support groups have sprung up all over the country. By meeting people in the same situation, grandparents get to swap stories and receive information about child management, financial aid, and various services that may be available. Often, the grandchildren get to meet and play together.

Many grandparents, although obliged to put parts of their lives on hold, have managed to preserve a little special time for themselves. One grandfather sat down with his wife to determine how much independent time they could have.

> "My wife made a list of our favorite activities that were unconnected with my little grandson. For now, we decided we'd each choose one. I picked my Saturday golf game, and she picked her Tuesday bridge club.
>
> "It's a good arrangement. We don't feel completely cut off from our own lives, and we are better able to enjoy our new 'Mom and Pop' role."

When You Are Not a Grandparent: But Would Like to Be

If you are not yet, or perhaps do not expect to be, a grandparent, it is natural to feel wistful, jealous, or unhappy at seeing your friends' families grow.

Do not deprive yourself of the pleasure of being with young children; do not deprive the children of the pleasure of being with you. Volunteer work involving children, foster grandparenting, interacting with the children of your relatives, friends, or neighbors can bring you much pleasure and satisfaction—both for yourself, and from the knowledge that you will be enriching a child's life.

Checklist: Points to Think About

- Be supportive to your child in his or her new role of parent.
- Follow the rules set by the parent.
- Avoid trying to be a "better" parent than your child.

- Avoid trying to be a "better" grandparent than the other grandparents.
- Avoid stepping between parent and child.
- Avoid criticizing your adult child in front of your grandchild.

Grandparenting Situations: Differences May Exist

When you have more than one grandchild, the dynamics of each relationship will be different. Do not feel concerned or dismayed. Various circumstances will determine the degree of your intimacy and involvement with each of them.

Geographic Proximity

You may have a different kind of closeness with the grandchild living ten minutes from you than with the one who lives an airplane ride away. The suggestions listed under "long-distance parenting" can be useful here.

First Grandchild

Some parents feel that a first anything has more wonder attached to it. Others do not. As has each of your children, each grandchild has a distinct personality. Your involvement can be different with each. Make each involvement special.

Daughter's or Son's Child

Are grandparents closer to a daughter's child than to a son's? Some say yes; others say no. Forget it, and enjoy your grandchild.

"Instant" Grandchild

If the young couple adopts a child, or there is a child from the spouse's previous marriage, it may take time for you to feel like a "real" grandparent. Do not rush the process. Gradually allow the child to enter your heart. You do not have to feel like a grandparent right away—or ever—in order to have a special relationship with that child. Be sensitive to the feelings of the child and the child's parents. Bestow gifts and other signs of your affection equally among your grandchildren.

Your grandchildren are not your children. You have a special relationship with them; you give them your time, your energy, and your love; you may *borrow* them for an hour, a day, a week. But—except for the situation where a grandparent is solely responsible for the children's upbringing—grandparents are not the primary force in their grandchildren's lives. Respect the wishes of their parents. Stay as much as possible within the parameters set by their parents.

Above all, enjoy your grandchildren—and love them, love them, love them!

Reflections

1. Think back to when you first became a parent and what you expected from your parents as grandparents.
   - Separate what it is you wish to duplicate and what you wish not to repeat.
   - Concentrate on the delicious, wonderful picture— warm, loving, full of fun—and make it happen.
2. Recall your grandparents or some substitute grandparent figure in your childhood.
   - What picture comes to your mind?
   - What experience do you cherish or savor?
   - What other pleasant remembrance appears?
3. Think back to when your children were young.
   - What were the positive aspects of your parents' role with your children?
   - Would you have wanted some changes?

- Would you have welcomed:
    More advice or support? Less?
    More baby-sitting or other help? Less?

Exercises

1. Questions to ask yourself:
    - Do you become over-zealous about the daily care of your grandchildren?
    - Are you critical of the way your adult children raise their children?
    - When asked, do you openly share with your children your experiences as a young parent so that they may adopt whatever they find useful?
    - Are you able to share your time and attention with your children and grandchildren so that you are satisfied, and they are, too?
    - Do you consult your children before you give your grandchildren a major gift?
    - Do you get agreement from your children before inviting the grandchildren to go somewhere with you?
2. If your answers to these questions left you feeling dissatisfied or uncomfortable, think about how you can change these answers—and your attitudes and actions.
3. Make a list: Write down what you would like to share and enjoy with a grandchild. Even very simple things can be special—a trip to the library, a game of cards, or a "mystery trip."

Remember: Make it fun for your grandchild—and yourself!

Chapter 9

Coping With Unconventional Lifestyles, Coping With Crisis

"My son, Gary, had been involved with drugs for years," said Eleanor, "but I didn't know it. Gary started borrowing money from his younger brother and sister when they were still in college. They gave him money from their allowances and their part-time jobs.

"Gary also went to his grandmother for money. My mother has since told me that she wanted Gary to tell me about it, but he looked so worried and nervous that she didn't insist.

"I did think that something was wrong—trouble with his job or an unhappy love affair. But I never dreamed of drugs. After all, Gary had his own apartment and his own life. I didn't see him too often.

"One day, I noticed that my mother was not wearing her diamond ring. When I mentioned it, her face got red and her hands shook. She had sold the ring, she said, to give the money to Gary. She had been giving him money for a long time."

When Eleanor spoke to her son, she heard a story that was more horrifying than she had imagined.

"Gary told me that his habit had gone beyond using drugs. He was selling them. And he was in debt. Way in debt. I couldn't believe it when he said that he needed three thousand dollars right away. If he didn't pay, he was in danger of being killed.

"Stunned is not strong enough a word to describe the way I felt. Gary cried, but I felt frozen. I told him to go home, that I needed time to think, that I'd talk to him the next day."

After Gary left, Eleanor pulled herself together and called her lawyer, the first person she thought of who could give her some professional advice and a possible referral. The lawyer told her that the best chance Gary had would be to register at a well-known drug rehabilitation center not far away. Eleanor also called Gary's father, who lived out of state.

The next day Eleanor confronted her son.

"I told him that I love him. 'Gary,' I said, 'this check in my hand is for three thousand dollars. You'll be able to clean up your debts *if* you sign yourself into the X-Y-Z Rehabilitation Center—by tomorrow.'

"Before he could utter a word, I put my hand on his shoulder. 'I have confidence in you, Gary. I know you'll lick this thing. But you must sign yourself into the center. Otherwise, I will tear up the check.' "

Eleanor had acted swiftly. This is very important in a case as severe as this, when parental love alone is not enough to bring about a change. Her first step had been to seek professional advice. Her lawyer directed her to the rehabilitation center, and from then on, her course of action was clear. Acting in a courageous and decisive way, she was able to convince her son to take the corrective steps to help himself.

What does a parent do when confronted with the unexpected, the painful, the unpleasant, or the tragic? There is no simple answer, but there are guidelines and general steps that you can follow.

Evaluate the Situation

Often, parents will pose the questions, "Why did this happen to me?" "What did I do wrong?" "Why do I deserve this?" Although these are understandable and common reactions to difficult situations, they rarely serve a useful purpose. When confronted with her son's predicament, Eleanor had no time to ask such questions, to "stay frozen," or to wring her hands. She had to plunge ahead, ignoring her fear. She knew she had to be quick, and she knew she had to be tough. Her son's life was threatened. Without the money, he might have been murdered. Just giving him the money without the accompanying condition would have perpetuated his self-destruction. She also would be participating in his wrongdoing. Eleanor faced the truth: This was a matter of life or death.

Not every problem is a matter of life or death, and most problems do not require the kind of split-second decision that Eleanor had to make; nor do they call for the degree of parental action that she took. Most problems should be worked out by the children themselves.

A parent can stand by with love and moral support, can give advice when asked, and can offer help when appropriate. It is vital for the parent to recognize that the responsibility for solving, alleviating, or living with the problem rests mainly with the adult child.

There are circumstances over which neither we nor our children have control: Accidents may occur, illness may strike, death may rob us of a loved one, divorce may tear a family apart. Situations involving life and death and severe illness are serious by anyone's standards, but many problems are not crises or catastrophes. This does not mean that you will be unaffected if a problem falls short of being life threatening, or that you will not be frightened or saddened or troubled.

One parent told this story:

> "My daughter is planning to marry an older man with two children. I'm very worried. I know it's my daughter's life and her decision, but I can't help feeling that she's making a big mistake.
>
> "At the very least, it's quite a different picture from what I always imagined. I guess I have to discard my dream."

Another parent said that she had not seen her son for two years.

> "We get a postcard every couple of months from various parts of the world. He has both business and mechanical skills and manages to find work whenever he needs it.
>
> "In the beginning, I worried myself sick over him. I've gotten to the point now where I can shove my worries to the back of my mind for periods of time. But I can't rid myself of the conviction that he's wasting his life—throwing it away. And I miss him. I keep looking at his photographs so that I won't forget what he looks like."

With the contemporary emphasis on individual fulfillment, we are presented with a great variety of lifestyles and situations. There may be communal living, or having a child out of wedlock, or having a way of life or an occupation "frowned upon" by convention. We each have our own standards, tastes, and values; what is not much more than an embarrassing lifestyle to one family may be perceived as a very serious problem to another. One parent deplores his child's choice of occupation; another applauds the identical choice.

Evaluate Your Role

You find yourself in a dilemma—how, when, or if you should be involved. Will you be helping or interfering? Will you be contributing to your child's welfare or stunting your child's emotional growth? Will you be taking on something that should be solely the adult child's responsibility? Are you fearful that if you take action, or withhold it, and then something goes wrong, you will be held responsible?

The reason for asking these questions is to avoid several pitfalls:

- Infantilizing your adult child
- Usurping your child's role or challenging his or her sense of responsibility
- Stepping between your child and your child's mate
- Creating, increasing, or perpetuating a dependency

As a parent, it is natural for you to react in some way to the disturbance in your child's life. Instead of responding impulsively, think about your role, if any, in what is happening.

A parent can choose to:

- Stand by.
- Express sympathy and understanding.
- Give advice upon request.

In which role would you be comfortable? Which role would fit your particular situation?

If disaster is imminent, as it was with Eleanor's drug-addicted son, a parent may have to become actively involved.

Define the Problem

Many problems fall into one of three categories:

• Shattering to parents' dreams
• Potentially dangerous
• Life threatening or similarly extreme

Your initial reaction to the suggestion of pigeonholing a problem may be, "Sure, it's easy for someone else to label the heartache that I'm going through." Even if it does not fall exactly into one of these categories, by labeling your problem you can eliminate some of the confusion that may surround it. You may be able to reduce some of its alarming properties.

Category 1: Shattering to Parents' Dreams

Sometimes your child's way of life is a problem not to him, but to you. You are the one who has to make the adjustment and deal with your anxiety and other concerns.

• Are you disappointed by your child's behavior?
• Do you feel humiliated or embarrassed?
• Is it difficult to acknowledge the situation to your friends and family?
• Is it difficult to acknowledge the situation to yourself?

Hal and his wife were very upset when their daughter separated from her husband.

"And," said Hal, "when Peggy told us that she had 'fallen in love' with someone from her office and had moved in with him, we were really shocked.

"Connie kept saying that she couldn't believe that our sweet little daughter, our Peggy, would live with a man who wasn't her husband. 'What will people think?' she said.

"I agreed that it would be embarrassing.

" 'How are we going to face everybody?' Connie asked."

We can all understand how Hal and Connie felt. There are also other emotions that a parent may experience—anger, disappointment, guilt, loss. One parent whose son was newly divorced spoke of her sadness at losing her daughter-in-law: "She was part of our family. I was sick at the thought of not seeing her anymore."

Another parent described how he felt about his son's change of career.

"My son was on his way to becoming a partner in his law firm," said Wayne, "and he chose to give it all up to grow herbs. He started out selling to nearby markets and has gradually established a thriving mail-order business.

"Whenever I reveal that I'm a little wistful about his old career, he just laughs and tells me how fulfilled he feels.

"I'm glad he's happy, but I still hem and haw when someone asks me what my son does. I find myself going into a long descripton of his success in his former law firm."

Adults, young or old, decide for themselves how to live their lives. Work toward accepting the choices your child has made.

Category 2: Potentially Dangerous

Sometimes you can foresee a crisis developing in your child's life. Your first impulse may be to jump right in and "rescue" your child. Or, you may want to deny the problem, put your head in the sand, and hold your breath until the problem goes away.

Instead of doing either, face the truth. Something is wrong or about to go wrong.

When Kate's husband died, she knew "deep down" that her son would take financial advantage of her. She tried to convince herself that he would change, that the death of his father would shock him into becoming more mature.

"My son, Roy, had always been an unconscionable spender," said Kate. "When my husband died, Roy moved into my house to 'take care' of me. He said he was going to devote himself to his writing.

"Instead, he devoted himself to sleeping until noon, and then going out drinking and gambling. He ran up all sorts of bills, and I paid them. Sure, Roy is weak and lazy, but he's my son and I love him.

"I told myself that this was only temporary, that things would get better. Well, they didn't get better—they got worse. And in no time at all, I lost a lot of money."

Kate told her son that she would no longer pay his bills.

"I said he could stay in the house until he found a job. This was a big mistake, and I knew it even while I was speaking. As long as he remained here, he would expect me to support him.

"After he indulged himself in several more spending sprees, I steeled myself and told him he had to go, job or not. It was a painful scene.

"I can't say he's 'reformed,' but he's better than he was. At least he has a job now, and a place to live. He knows he has to work or he won't be able to pay his rent. And, so far, he hasn't asked me for money."

By admitting to herself that her son was unreliable and irresponsible, Kate finally faced reality. Roy's behavior would have eventually destroyed her financial security.

By insisting that he move out, Kate helped both her son and herself. She gave her son an opportunity to grow up, and she took herself out of financial jeopardy.

Roy's conduct directly involved both himself and his mother, but most times parents observe something happening in their child's life—not theirs.

What if it is not you but your child who is in denial?

Lenore knew that her son-in-law was a gambler, and she knew that her daughter skimped and scraped to keep the household together. Lenore had tried to broach the subject several times, but was always rebuffed by her daughter.

"I could never give Brooke any money," said Lenore, "even when I said it was strictly for the kids. Brooke always said she didn't need it. She insisted that she was okay.

"One day I dropped in when the children were eating lunch. My two-year-old grandson was crying. Before Brooke could speak, my four-year-old granddaughter looked up and said, "Jackie's crying because he wants more bread. He's bad. He knows there's only one piece of bread for lunch. I know that.'

"I looked at Brooke, but she had turned away. I went straight to the refrigerator. It was almost empty. On the top shelf was a jar of bluish liquid.

" 'Is that supposed to be milk?' I asked. 'What's happening, Brooke? You're putting water in the milk? And you're rationing the children's bread? Is this some kind of war you're fighting?' "

Lenore's daughter finally admitted that there was very little money for food. She shielded her husband from blame, saying that he tried not to gamble, but couldn't help himself. She was trying to get the children into a day care center so that she could go to work.

"I didn't know what to do," said Lenore. "I gave Brooke some money for food. I practically had to beg her to take it."

Ultimately, Lenore's daughter placed the children in a day care center. She found a part-time job and was able to, in Lenore's words, "give Jackie two slices of bread for lunch."

What can you do when confronted by a situation involving your child's or grandchild's health? As Lenore did, you can confront your child with the truth. If your child denies the truth, refuses to discuss it, or makes all kinds of excuses, you can suggest ways for him or her to leave the situation or to improve it.

- Offer temporary shelter, love, and emotional support.
- Suggest professional help—such as Gamblers Anonymous or Alcoholics Anonymous.
- Suggest a "surrogate parent"—perhaps a mutual friend (ideally your child's contemporary), someone your child trusts and respects and can talk to. (Your child at this time may balk at seeking professional help.)

The purpose of a parent's intervention should not be to change a child's beliefs or lifestyle, but to support the child in extricating himself or herself from difficult or dangerous circumstances, and to protect any young children involved.

- Help your child to acknowledge the problem.
- Express your fear that your child is headed for disaster.
- Avoid degrading your child; avoid speaking in a disrespectful or patronizing way; avoid giving orders.
- Make positive recommendations for him to take responsibility and turn his path around.

The parent can assess the situation, decide what kind of problem it is, and if there is danger to the child—or anyone else.

- If you see impending danger, warn your child. When? Immediately. When you see it, say it!
- Encourage your child to acknowledge the problem and to take the steps to turn his path around.
- Beware of "over-helping" your child. "Helping" sometimes masks a desire to control. Learn when to back off!

Sometimes parents know that something is wrong, but cannot, or will not, face their fears. Russ and Isabelle had come to terms with their son's homosexuality when Evan was still in his teens. They had gone through all the stages of denial, anger, and, finally, acceptance. Because Evan's lifestyle was no longer an issue with them, they were able to wholeheartedly express their love and support for their son. Recently, Isabelle noticed that there was a lot of tension between Russ and herself.

"Russ and I began quarreling with each other," said Isabelle. "The silliest thing could spark a fight. I guess I really did know what was happening with us, but I just couldn't acknowledge it, even to myself.

"Things got so bad that we made an appointment to see a therapist."

In the process of therapy, the underlying problem came to light. They were terrified that their son could contract AIDS. What would happen to him? What could they do? How could they help?

"The therapist," said Russ, "helped us to look at things in a fairly objective way. We had both been so frightened that we'd turned our fear into anger. We were angry at Evan—for being in such a vulnerable and dangerous situation. We were angry at Evan—but we could not admit it, and so we turned the anger on ourselves and fought with each other.

"Following the therapist's advice, we called an AIDS hotline and armed ourselves with all kinds of information. Then, we were ready to speak to Evan.

"I never would have believed it, but that talk opened the floodgates. Evan knew all along that we were worried, but couldn't bring himself to broach the subject.

"We discussed a lot of things. He reassured us that he and his partner were aware of the dangers and were taking appropriate measures to ensure good health.

"It's such a relief to be truthful with each other."

By seeking therapy and equipping themselves with knowledge about AIDS, Isabelle and Russ were able to break their silence, admit their fears, and express their concerns to their son.

Category 3: Life-threatening

Vivian's son, Tim, had been diagnosed as being HIV positive. Some time ago, Tim had undergone emergency treatment for a bleeding ulcer. The treatment had involved several blood transfusions. It later was discovered that the blood was infected with the AIDS virus.

Vivian has had to be supportive not only of Tim, but of Tim's wife as well.

"I try to be strong and help my son and my daughter-in-law," said Vivian, "but it's been rough. And I must say that I found out things about people that I really didn't want to know. I guess they're frightened, or embarrassed, or they just don't know. That doesn't help me or my family.

"Some friends I thought would stand by us have just melted away. And one said to me, 'I guess Tim got it from his college days. They all used drugs then, didn't they?' Without meaning to, I kept finding myself on the defen-

sive, telling all who would listen that Tim had been infected with tainted blood."

Like Isabelle and Russ, Vivian knew she needed information
and advice. Tim's doctor referred her to a local support group
for the families of AIDS patients.

"The group has been very helpful. I've learned about the
disease. I've learned how to help Tim without babying him
or moaning about what bad luck he's had. And, very
important, I've learned to plan activities for the days he
feels better.
"I've shared this knowledge with my daughter-in-law.
She's such a sweet girl. We've always liked each other, and
now we're closer than ever. We try to cheer each other up.
And sometimes Tim is the one who cheers us up."

Another positive result Vivian obtained from the support
group was meeting people in similar situations.

"I was so impressed with their courage. One woman in
particular was so brave, so truthful. She told me how she
went through all the stages of suffering—how she was so
angry at her daughter, how she had blamed her for getting
AIDS, and how she was able to move through her anger
and give her love to her child.
"I learned so much. I learned how to express my gratitude to my friends who were supportive and loving—and
even to forgive the people who deserted us."

Extreme problems defy easy solutions. There are times when
you must face a problem head on and take some kind of action;
there are times when you must learn to live with the problem;
there are times when you must behave in a way that is at odds
with your personality.

After a false start, Enid found the way to help her child face his problem by himself.

"Andy had gotten in with a wild crowd," said Enid, "and took part in a robbery. We were all devastated. Andy had been doing so well at his job, and now he was sure that his career was over.

"Andy was sentenced to a year and a half in jail. We wrote him long letters, saying that he would be out soon, that everything was going to be all right. I assured him that we understood, and that his boss would understand, too, and give him his job back when the sentence was finished.

"It was not until Andy asked me to call up his boss and beg him to save the job for him that I realized what I had been doing. I had been helping to keep Andy from taking responsibility for his behavior. I had actually been implying that it was all right that Andy had robbed someone, that it was all right that he was a convicted criminal! I was appalled at myself."

Enid and her husband continued to write letters and visit their son all through the long months of his sentence. They told him they loved him, but they no longer offered him useless sympathy for his plight, nor did they encourage him to complain.

"In the beginning," said Enid, "Andy used to complain about the food and the inmates and everything else about the prison, and we always agreed with him. But after we saw that we were not helping him, we stopped doing this.

"In our letters and during our visits, we spoke of law and order and civic responsibility. We also spoke of family matters, current events, and books. We wanted to keep him in touch with the outside world, to let him know that there *was* an outside world, and that he would be part of it again.

"This was ten years ago. Andy has been straight ever since. It took him quite a while to find work when he came out—his former boss would not answer his calls—but Andy didn't lose hope. He has a decent job now, and we consider him—and he considers himself—a respectable citizen."

It may not always be possible to encourage your child to take full responsibility—first for his or her situation, and then for the steps needed to solve or mitigate the problem. There may be a situation when you cannot talk with your child, when you have to use your own judgment, perhaps in conjunction with professional help.

Years ago, Paul's daughter ran off to join a cult.

"My wife and I could not get in touch with Donna," Paul said. "We were not allowed to visit her. Our letters were returned unopened. We were desperate, ready to go to any lengths to rescue her. We hired a man who had been very successful in getting kids out of these cults.

"It was a nightmare from start to finish, but it would have been more of a nightmare to lose Donna forever.

"When she was finally home with us, she was like a zombie. It took a lot of therapy and a lot of love, but things are better now."

Another parent in a similar situation tried various means of getting his son back—writing to him, sending family photographs, visiting him when the organization allowed—but he stopped short of using force.

"Kidnap my own child?" said Joseph. "No, that's not for me. We've been able to see him about twice a year. He seems content.

"Maybe someday a miracle will happen, and he'll come back to our world. Anyway, we've made peace with ourselves and, I think, with our son. The most important point for me is that I feel we've left the door open."

Similar problems, different methods of approach. Each family acted in a way that was compatible with its own attitudes and beliefs.

There may come a time when a parent has to recognize that an adult child is going to go through an experience alone. Joseph seemed to realize this instinctively. He could not bring himself to use force. He took comfort in the hope that one day his son would return home.

Sometimes the parent's decision to back off, to remain uninvolved, will give the adult child enough space and strength to work out his problem alone and thereby gain a feeling of his own power.

Facing the Truth

Telling yourself the truth and acknowledging the problem—as painful as that may be—are the first steps in tackling the problem. Avoid whitewashing the facts; avoid telling yourself that "everything will be all right—as long as I'm hopeful and optimistic things will get better." Hope and optimism are marvelous qualities to have; they can do wonders for your life. By all means cultivate them. But hope and optimism are not substitutes either for truth or for action. They should not be used to lull you into thinking that nothing need be done. Serious problems seldom go away by themselves. Left alone, they can become more serious.

For a long time, Marilyn had always "looked away" whenever she saw signs of her daughter's alcoholism.

"I chose not to believe it," said Marilyn. "I told myself that Karen was a social drinker. She liked people and she liked parties. So what if she took an extra drink once in a while?

"But I began to feel that something was wrong. Karen had always been so articulate and friendly, so neat and clean. One day I noticed that she looked actually dirty, as if she hadn't taken a shower in days. She seemed a different person to me, sullen and edgy. When I asked her if something was wrong, she lost her temper and screamed, 'Don't pick on me. I'm not a child.' "

That night, Marilyn thought about her encounter with her daughter and admitted to herself that Karen had been drunk.

"But I still wasn't ready to face it. I told myself that Karen wouldn't drink more than she could handle. I told myself that I probably imagined everything and that things would be all right.

"A week later, driving home from a party, Karen smashed her car into a tree. She broke her nose, her arm, and her collarbone.

"Karen was charged with drunk driving and was given a long period of probation."

Marilyn told us about the economic and other consequences of Karen's alcoholism. Karen's medical insurance company did not cover her medical bills, nor did her car insurance company cover her automobile repair bills.

"Karen had to junk the car," said Marilyn. "She wouldn't have been able to drive it anyway, because her driver's license was revoked for a year.

"Karen needed transportation for her medical visits and therapy sessions. She also needed it when she went back to work.

"The bills kept piling up. The medical costs were staggering. We took out a loan to help her. We all took turns driving her to work—my husband and I and her brother tried to be as helpful as possible, but it's been a big strain on everybody.

"It's five years since the accident. Karen has almost finished paying us back for the money we spent on her bills."

Marilyn had ignored the signs of impending danger; she had refused to acknowledge to herself that her daughter was an alcoholic. She was lucky. Her daughter's story could have turned out differently. Karen suffered relatively minor injuries, and she did not hurt anyone else.

Admitting that a problem exists can be the first step you take in encouraging your child to deal with it.

Extreme situations require professional advice. This is certainly true when dealing with eating disorders.

Mitchell and his wife were always careful not to interfere in their children's lives. However, something was happening to their daughter that they could not ignore. Shari was so obsessed with the fear of getting fat that she put herself on a starvation diet. When the family went out to dinner, Mitchell noticed that she ate nothing more than a few carrot sticks. Her parents begged her to see her doctor, but she absolutely refused. They finally spoke to their own doctor, who referred them to a psychologist who specialized in treating eating disorders.

"Shari wouldn't go," said Mitchell. "We pleaded, we bribed, we cried. She kept telling us there was no problem, that she looked great, that it was all in our minds—we were imagining the whole thing. Meanwhile, she was getting so skinny you could see every bone."

Mitchell and his wife were frightened. They decided to consult the psychologist themselves.

"The psychologist advised us to use intervention. We had to steel ourselves to adopt a method alien to our normal behavior. We discussed the matter with members of our family—our son, our older daughter, and my father-in-law.

"Together we confronted Shari. We told her we knew what was happening. She was deluding herself. She was not fat. She looked like a skeleton—a Holocaust survivor. We told her she was killing herself, and that she herself had to do something about it.

"Strong words. Painful words. We were all emotionally drained. But it worked! Shari burst into tears and agreed to see the psychologist."

Parents whose children suffer from anorexia (starving oneself) and bulimia (bingeing and purging) are often overcome with guilt—at having given their daughters too much food in childhood (eating disorders usually affect young women), or having given them the wrong food, or having forced them to eat, or having forced them to do *anything*. Mothers especially feel this way. What is so basic to our lives as FOOD? And who is so traditionally associated with food as MOTHER?

Therapy revealed causes for Shari's behavior that had nothing to do with food. Mitchell and his wife sought therapy for themselves to learn how to deal with their own feelings of inadequacy and guilt, and to learn how to help their daughter as she started to heal herself.

Admitting the truth—as painful as that may be—is the first step in tackling a problem. Sometimes a parent's denial can be so strong that he tries to convince himself that an ominous situation is normal.

"I knew my son-in-law was temperamental," said George. "I knew he could be rough sometimes. But my daughter seemed okay.

"When I saw Susie with a swollen arm, I believed her when she said she had tripped on a step. But my wife and I began to notice that Susie didn't laugh and joke anymore. She looked as if she did a lot of crying.

"My wife suspected that my son-in-law was pushing Susie around. She wanted to say something, but I persuaded her—and myself—that he would never do that, and that it would be better if Susie worked out her problems by herself. I felt we shouldn't interfere."

George kept denying that anything was seriously wrong until the day he unexpectedly met his daughter in the supermarket parking lot.

"The minute Susie saw me, she raised her hand to shield the left side of her face.
"I couldn't believe what I saw. She had a black eye!
" 'You didn't trip on a step this time,' I said.
"She started to cry and admitted that her husband had hit her. He'd been hitting her for some time. She hadn't known what to do. She was too ashamed to tell us."
"I felt enraged. This man had abused my daughter! I was also furious with myself for having tried to sweep everything under the rug. I took my child in my arms, and told her, 'Come home with me.' "

Denial was no longer possible for George, nor was passive behavior. He had no choice but to get involved. He encouraged his daughter to find an attorney who was experienced in the area of marital physical abuse. He also helped her locate a support group so that she could start to help herself.

Dealing With the Situation

Determine the Nature of the Problem

Try to separate your love for your child from the problem, and to separate yourself emotionally from it. Review in your mind the three categories: shattering to parents' dreams, potentially dangerous, and life threatening. Armed with this set of criteria, and using it as your guide, determine the degree or nature of your child's situation.

- Does the situation involve your emotions?
- Does it require some sort of adjustment—either by you or by your child?
- Does it involve life or death, or a less threatening but still serious illness?
- Does it involve the law?
- Does it hurt your child, Physically or emotionally? Your grandchildren? You? Other members of the family?

It truly may be a crisis, requiring your (or someone else's) intervention or assistance. Or it may be a difficult situation that can be surmounted, helped, or lived with once you give it thought and understanding, love and patience. Or it may be walking the fine line between potential danger and crisis. The impending danger may be obvious, or not. You may sense that something is wrong without actually being told about it. There are times when you have nothing to go on but an intuitive knowledge about your child, plus an inner sense of anxiety that will not go away.

It is pointless to try to stifle anxiety. No matter how hard you ignore or deny it, parts of your intuitive knowledge will trickle down into your subconscious—into your thoughts, your behavior, your dreams. Pay attention to it. Anxiety or uneasiness can serve a useful purpose. As George realized after he saw his daughter's black eye, a parent's uneasiness can be a warning of danger. George said that, afterward, he kept thinking of his daughter's dangerous position.

"During all that time Susie was in trouble, I just didn't want to face the possibility of such a thing. I'm thankful I was there that day and saw what she looked like. Who knows what might have happened if things went on that way? That time it was a black eye. Next time it could have been a brain concussion."

Discuss the Problem With Someone: Seek Advice

Speak to a close friend or colleague—someone you trust and respect. Not only may you get some fresh ideas from that person, but as you speak about the problem, you may view it differently. Also, enlist the views, cooperation, and aid of your children, family members, and other people who are willing and capable of giving helpful support. Speaking to a friend whose child had been in a similar situation might be useful.

Eleanor sought help from a lawyer about her drug-addicted son; Mitchell sought help from a psychologist about his anorexic daughter.

You might consult professionals—as did Eleanor and Mitchell. Your source can be a lawyer, doctor, psychologist, clergyman—a person who has knowledge and information, and whose judgment you trust. You might seek counsel for yourself—as Isabelle and Russ did.

A word of caution: Dealing with other people's reactions is not always easy. Be prepared for the possibility that even your closest, dearest friends—because of different experiences in their lives—may respond quite differently from you and may offer unwelcome comments. You don't have to explain your own views, nor do you need to be defensive about yourself or your child. If you wish, you can simply acknowledge your friend's concern and thank him or her for it.

On the other hand, you can treat these comments and opinions as opportunities to think about the issue more clearly. These comments may contain some truth; might some of them be valid for you?

Discuss the Problem With Your Child

Start by concentrating on the problem itself; then discuss ways that it might be resolved. Recognize, and communicate to your child, that you cannot solve the problem. It is up to your child to take the responsibility for dealing with it.

Be aware of your child's personality—of what can cause provocation or adverse reactions. Be prepared for his or her responses, for negative reactions, surprises, and the need for negotiation. You need not rehearse an entire conversation, but do give some prior thought to what you can say to engage your troubled child in a two-way dialogue. Focus on those aspects that are positive and that will lead to trust, cooperation, and constructive action.

- Speak openly, frankly.
- Tell the truth as you see it.
- Avoid being judgmental.
- Avoid the use of such phrases as:
  "How could you do such a thing?"
  "I knew this would happen. I told you so."

Your emotions can cloud your judgment and your ability to speak and act objectively. Be aware of this. With preparation, you are more likely to reach a good level of communication. As you speak, be sensitive to what is "going on" with your child. Be prepared to alter your original script in order to keep the communication going.

- Aim for objectivity.
- Discuss the problem as quietly and unemotionally as you can.
- Clarify the problem together if possible.
- Evaluate the problem together.

Without a lot of emotional baggage, your child can start to consider the situation and begin to deal with it.

Ask your child if he or she has considered other options. Suggest some, bearing in mind that the child must assume responsibility for the choice.

Avoid searching for scapegoats. How easy it is in a troubled situation to look for someone or something to blame—your child, yourself, your spouse, your child's friends. Instead, encourage your child to find ways of overcoming the problem, express your confidence that he is capable of doing so, and show your own willingness to be helpful.

When you're in conversation with your child about a serious problem, be a good listener.

- Aim for a dialogue with your child, not a monologue.
- Avoid needless interruptions.
- Avoid monopolizing the conversation.
- Encourage your child to express fully his or her opinions and wishes.
- Share your fears. Instead of a flat "You're wrong," substitute, "I'm concerned; have you thought about what will happen if . . . ?"
- Share your feelings. If you withhold your feelings in order not to burden your child, and if you act *too* reserved, your child may think that you do not care. If you feel troubled or frightened, say so.
- Be direct; be honest; be realistic. If you automatically say, "Don't worry, everything will be all right," you are downplaying the actual problem, the child's responsibility for the problem, and the need for the child to take that responsibility.
- Recognize your child's pain or sense of loss.
- Show your sympathy and offer solace.

You can make it clear that, although you may not agree with your child's lifestyle, you still accept your child as a person. The words, "I love you," sincerely said and wholeheartedly meant, can go a long way to smooth over difficult times.

- Together, discuss the various choices or solutions available.
- Discuss the necessity or advisability of getting appropriate legal or medical advice.
- Discuss your child's role in solving or dealing with the problem.

- Discuss the appropriateness of a role for you.
- Avoid overreacting—with emotional responses, help, or advice.

Discuss Plans

Look for opportunities to help your adult children to take charge of their own lives, so that they will make better choices and take more responsibility for their actions.

It can be difficult to refrain from jumping right in and trying to solve the problem. "Don't worry," you may have said when your child was very young, "everything will be all right." But now, you are no longer the parent of a six-year-old, kissing away the hurt. Now, everything may not be all right, and it may be inappropriate to tell your adult child not to worry. It is more appropriate now to help the young adult face the problem. It might even be better for you to stand by and watch—while still being available if needed.

Enid came to realize that she had been infantilizing her son by not addressing his wrongdoing. Fortunately, she changed her attitude and communicated to her son the necessity for facing up to what he had done.

Before you offer help or a plan of action, be clear in your own mind as to what it is you are prepared to do. Be frank. Explain what and how much help you are prepared to offer. Act in a way that reflects or conforms to your own convictions and beliefs, one that allows you to keep your own sense of integrity.

A father was asked by his daughter to help her with her divorce proceedings. She wanted him to exaggerate some facts about her husband's behavior. Initially, he agreed. He had always found it hard to say no to his daughter. After thinking it over, he realized that he felt uncomfortable and decided not to compromise his integrity. He told his daughter that he could not do what she asked. "I will help you get a good lawyer, and I will stand by you during this difficult period in your life."

Maintain a Positive Attitude

While still keeping in touch with reality, be as upbeat and positive as you can. When dealing with an overwhelming problem, break it down into segments that can be handled more easily. A positive attitude will help you and your child create a climate of family love and support.

Help Yourself

If you give a problem free rein, it can quickly dominate all of your time and energy. Aim for a healthy balance in your life. It is normal to feel sad some of the time. Allow yourself to cry, but do not let all the weight be on one side of the seesaw of life. You need some pleasure occasionally. It will boost your energy and provide a bit of emotional relief.

Take a Break

One parent said that whenever she felt very depressed she would take a shower and—scream. "I find the shower a good place for privacy. I go in there and scream and cry and let the water mingle with my tears. It doesn't change the situation, but I come out feeling lighter somehow—and better able to cope."

Seek out ways to have a good time. If possible, plan to "escape" for a day or a weekend. If that is more freedom than your schedule will permit, read a book, see a movie, take a long walk; or work out at a health club or gym, a tennis court, a golf course. Declare this period of time to be off-limits for thinking about your troubles. Constant grieving wears you out and destroys your ability to think clearly.

It may not be possible to change or eliminate the problem.

One parent took great comfort from a saying of her father's: "If you can't solve a problem, try to let go of it."

Shake Off Negative Feelings and Thoughts

Consider what the situation is doing to your life and your relationships. Avoid seeing yourself as a victim: "Why did this happen to me? Life is not fair." True, life is not fair. Life just *is*. Neither "life" nor your children conspire to make you miserable.

Some people feel that suffering is a part of being a concerned parent. Moreover, they feel they have to show that they are suffering.

Lola's experience is a common one.

"I hadn't gone anywhere in months," said Lola. "One day my friend dragged me to a movie. It was a comedy and, before I knew it, I was laughing out loud along with everyone else. When I realized it, I clamped my hand over my mouth and looked around to see if anybody noticed.

"My child is going through a bitter custody battle—I'm in danger of having my grandchildren dragged off to a distant state—and here I am, in a movie house, laughing and having fun."

Reject the idea that you have to suffer in order to be a caring, concerned parent.

- Avoid feeling guilty.
- Help yourself to achieve a positive attitude. That in itself will be helpful to your child.
- Consider seeking counseling for yourself—to restore your morale and to learn how to interact with your child.

Seek out upbeat, enthusiastic people. Avoid those who are

always gloomy and pessimistic, and who, while commiserating with you, constantly talk about your problem.

As a concerned and loving parent, it is comforting to feel that you are there when needed—to give help if asked, to step in if necessary, and to offer strength by just standing by. An even greater comfort can be yours when you see your adult child solving and surmounting the problem, and when you know that whatever happens, that if you are not there—if you "turn your head away"; if you are working, on vacation, or otherwise involved with your own concerns; and when you die—your child is a mature individual, able to stand alone and take responsibility for his or her own life. Is this not the essence of "letting go," the essence of seeing your adult child truly grown up?

Exercises

There is no formula, no easy answer, no sure way to solve or alleviate a painful or serious situation. But by reviewing some of the already-mentioned suggestions, you can create some guidelines that will be appropriate for you and your child.

1. Identify the problem.
2. Put it in its proper category. Is it:
   • Shattering to your dreams?
   • Potentially dangerous?
   • Life threatening?
3. Evaluate the problem, not the person. Try to view it clearly and unemotionally.
4. Review the problem. Can it be solved, overcome, alleviated, lessened? If not, how can you coexist with it?
5. Talk to a trusted friend.
6. Consult a professional. Discuss what reasonable goals you can set.
7. Talk with your child. Be sensitive to his or her needs. When asked, be prepared with alternate recommendations.

8. Be aware of your own personality and style of communicating.
9. Refrain from speaking hastily. If you find that you are overreacting, pull back.
10. Listen when your child speaks. Aim for a dialogue—not a monologue. A true give-and-take—not a lecture.
11. Support your child in his efforts to start the action going. Discuss with your child the need for outside help. If this is impractical or impossible, you may have to proceed on your own.

Chapter 10

When Parents' Lives Change: Widowhood, Divorce, Remarriage

Becoming widowed or divorced, remarrying or remaining single may each seem separate and unique states of being, but common problems and circumstances run through them.

Sad times come to all of us—sad times, unhappy times, uncomfortable times. Tranquility, peace, and even joy can be coaxed out of many a difficult situation. Knowing that sad times come and go, and that other, better times await us, we can start to heal ourselves and deal with our sadness and our pain.

Misfortune and sorrow enter everyone's life, but compensations exist, too. With an open mind and a willingness to adapt to the changes in our lives, we can transform these compensations into advantages.

Widowhood

Handling the initial loss of a mate usually brings the family together in a positive way, physically and emotionally. But not always. Following the initial trauma, grief can cause people to react in negative ways toward one another.

When you are first widowed, a grieving period is necessary. The comforts of marriage, the happiness, the feeling of security, have vanished. In addition, you may be faced with a multitude of practical problems and readjustments. Your friends and your children may suddenly perceive you as a different person. Newly single, you may perceive yourself differently. Notice how you react to your situation. Be aware of what you expect from your friends and relatives, and from your adult children. People may cluster around you, offering love and emotional support. Be receptive to this support; open your heart to it; don't push people away. If you need assistance, learn to accept graciously the help and love offered you, without feeling that you are being taken over.

You need time, too—time to be alone, to think, to "find yourself." Thought is the forefather of action: First we think, then we plan, then we act.

As the remaining spouse, needing to deal with reality, you may experience a feeling of strength and independence, or you may surrender to grief and despair. The children may respond with love and support toward you, or, out of their own grief and fear, may express impatience and anger.

One man described a harrowing situation. After his wife died, his son and daughter accused him of neglect.

> "They said I called the specialist too late," said Jack. "They accused me of everything from being cheap to being callous and selfish. They brought up old stories and old fights from years ago. I thought I'd been to the depths with my wife's illness, but this was even worse. My children wouldn't see me or speak to me."

Obviously, the bitterness of Jack's children was not a sudden occurrence. Upon further discussion, Jack admitted that he had not been the best of fathers, or the best of husbands. He decided to take action. He attended counseling sessions for several months, and, as a result, he wrote letters to his children. He did not try to whitewash the past, nor did he make excuses for himself.

"I told my kids that I loved them. I asked them to try to forgive me for all that had happened. I asked them if we could start afresh. I told them I needed them and hoped that in some way they needed me."

The reconciliation between Jack and his children was unexpectedly quick. The children had been suffering remorse, too, and welcomed, albeit cautiously, the chance to get to know their father and to learn how to be a family.

As we have seen, an adult child may accuse the surviving parent of not having been helpful or caring enough in the past. Similarly, a parent may accuse a child of various misdeeds. Or a child may accuse a sibling. Or the surviving parent may be a *self-accuser*, tormented by real or perceived guilt. Or the surviving parent may feel anger and resentment for all the difficult times spent caring for the now deceased spouse.

The feelings and accusations can be acknowledged and the situation explained. Perhaps a grain of truth exists in the accusations; or the allegations are wholly false; or the situation has been misunderstood; or facts that until now were hidden can be finally revealed. Jack acted wisely on several points. He knew he could not handle the situation alone, and so he sought professional help. When he was ready to contact his children, he did not immediately try to see them, but wrote to them, thereby giving *them* the opportunity to take the initiative. In his letters, he did not try to exonerate himself; in a straightforward way, he told them of his love and his need for them.

Financial Arrangements

Finances may take center stage at this time. The paperwork surrounding the altered status of the widowed partner can seem overwhelming to the whole family. In their desire to help, the adult children may rush in to take care of various financial details and overwhelm the surviving parent. Or, for various reasons, the children may not wish or may not be able to become involved.

The time-honored cliché of the woman who never balanced her checkbook, who knew neither where her money was invested nor the name of her stockbroker, is not as archaic as might be supposed. Too often one partner manages financial matters to the exclusion of the other partner. Such lack of involvement is not necessarily limited to the wife.

The use of the computer to handle personal finances can complicate matters. If both partners are knowledgeable about the family's finances, but only one partner operated the computer, the other partner may not know how to retrieve the stored information.

Before panic sets in, assess the situation as objectively as possible. What has to be done? Is it just a matter of organizing records and receipts, or are there masses of papers lying around in great disarray, coupled with unpaid bills, dunning letters, and final notices? Does ownership of various accounts and securities have to be changed?

Do you wish to involve your children in organizing your finances? Do you want their advice, or do you want them to oversee or actually do the job?

If the job is overwhelming, or if you do not wish to do it, consider getting professional help. There are financial services that offer bookkeepers or accountants on a weekly or monthly basis to organize your finances and keep them running smoothly. One woman called in a free-lance financial consultant who set up a computer-based financial system for her.

"Best thing I ever did," said Helene. "I was always involved in handling our finances, but I worked with my husband. We worked together. Now, all at once, I had this chore facing me, and I thought that maybe I should learn to use a computer.

"The expert I hired was great. She came once a week for

three months, talked me through the computer, and helped me set up a budget and a bookkeeping system. As a result of the new skills I learned, I felt more in control.

"But most of all, I was freed from having to ask my children how to set up this kind of system. Now when we come together, we enjoy ourselves instead of having to deal with the computer and discuss finances."

Developing new skills is always empowering. Learning to use the computer in order to manage her finances gave Helene a sense of independence and enabled her to go on with other aspects of her life without fear and without being tied to her adult children's schedules.

Living Arrangements

Physical living arrangements are often evaluated at this time. "You can't live alone," a child may tell the widowed parent. Or the widowed parent may come to the same conclusion.

Counselors often recommend that, if possible, no change in living arrangements should be made for about a year. The widowed partner needs time to deal with grief, to adjust to living without the deceased spouse, and to get financial and other matters in order.

When and If to Make a Move

Are your present living conditions physically uncomfortable? Do they provoke painful memories? On a more positive note, do you wish to move in order to simplify your life, such as going from a house into a more manageable apartment? Do you wish to move into a different and perhaps more interesting neighborhood?

Assess the situation:

- What will you gain by moving?
- Will the new living quarters be easy to maintain?

- Is the new location convenient in terms of transportation, shops, and various places of interest?
- Will you be able to maintain your independence at the new location?
- Will you still be near friends and family?
- Will you be near places where you will have the opportunity to make new acquaintances, such as colleges or other centers of learning?

Moving Near One's Child

If your adult children live a long distance from you, carefully weigh all the factors involved before considering pulling up your own roots in order to move nearby.

- Do you view the move as a challenge and an adventure, or as a last resort, something to stave off loneliness or financial difficulty?
- Do you have a close circle of friends and an absorbing vocation or hobby in your present location?
- Are you willing to work at making new friends and exploring vocations and hobbies in the new location?

Another factor to consider is how entrenched your child is in his or her present living arrangement. One man told us that when his wife died, he sold his apartment in Florida and moved to St. Louis to be near his son and daughter-in-law.

> "It took me a while to settle in, but eventually I got used to it. And then, two years later, my son was transferred to Chicago. What was I supposed to do, uproot myself again? I moved back to Florida."

If you are thinking about relocating, and each of your children lives in a different part of the country, will your choice of one place over another cause friction between your children? (Your children may be arguing over you. It may even be going this way: "You take him!" "No, *you* take him!")

Calm, rational discussion is needed. Now is the time for total honesty, without any attempt to soft-pedal the reasons that your adult children want you to move near them. Frequently, we hear parents say that their children need them for baby-sitting and moral support. One woman called it "oatmeal cookie backup."

"I knew from the start that both my daughters wanted me to move near them—five hundred miles away," said Gina. "It wasn't a question of money or baby-sitting. They and their husbands all have good jobs and good child care arrangements. But they wanted the added security of knowing that if the sitter got sick, or one of the children got sick, I'd be with a pot of soup and a plate of my famous cookies.

"This happened shortly after my husband's death. We were all still pretty shaky and really didn't know what to do.

"I decided that I would make no drastic changes for at least a year. What I've been doing is visiting each of them from time to time for a week or so.

"It's worked out well. It's been more than a year now, and I've decided not to move. I love to visit my children and grandchildren, and they love to have me. But I'm also comfortable with my life at home. Little by little, I've gotten used to living alone."

By taking her time in deciding if she wanted to move, Gina was able to enjoy the companionship of her family while she was making up her mind. When she was finally ready, she was able to make the right decision—for her.

If Gina had decided to move far away to be near her daughters, she would have been doing so by choice, not out of fear of being alone or in response to her children's requests.

If you are in a similar position to Gina's, try to make your decision in as leisurely and deliberate a fashion as she did.

Consider why your children want you to move—extra baby-sitting or other child care, house repairs, cooking for the working couple, emotional help, friendship, companionship.

Consider the pros and the cons of your present life. Do the same thing for your life if you have already moved. It is natural to want to live near your children and to help them if you can, but consider first, and very seriously, your own needs and desires. They may or may not concur with your children's requests.

Moving in With One's Child

"My daughter has a large house," said Janice, "and she wants to carve out a small apartment for me. She's even planning a little kitchen there.

"I don't know what to do. Part of me is tempted. My daughter and son-in-law and I are on excellent terms, and, of course, it would be wonderful to see my grandchildren all the time, but I keep remembering that old saying, 'You never really know someone until you live with that person.'

"Do I really want to live in the same house with my children, even though I would have my own apartment?

"It's true that I have frequent periods of loneliness now, but would I feel any less lonely living with them? And would I be giving up part of my independence? I can almost hear Mary Lou asking me why I came home so late last night. I like to come and go as I please, and I'm not looking for role-reversal with my daughter.

"It's been many years since I've had a day-to-day involvement with her.

"Would our present relationship be difficult to maintain if we lived under one roof?"

Janice's words clearly revealed her reluctance to move in with her daughter. But, on the other hand, sometimes such an arrangement can be mutually satisfactory to all involved. For another woman, moving in with her son and daughter-in-law turned out to be a positive force in her life.

"Everyone warned me not to do it," said Roberta, "and I was very uncertain about it, too. But the advantages seemed to outweigh any disadvantages.

"My daughter-in-law is a very intelligent person. She's also rather blunt. We sat down, just the two of us, and brought up every issue we could think of. We worked out a financial plan, whereby I would pay a monthly amount, rather than itemize individual expenses.

"Then, we called in my son and discussed everything with him. We even talked about my moving out if it didn't work out.

"Well, it has worked out. The house is large. I have my own room and my own bathroom. We live right in town, so I can walk to the stores and the library. I feel independent and, little by little, I've gotten a social life for myself. And, of course, I'm so happy to be such a close part of my grandchildren's lives.

"But, above all, the reason everything's worked out so well is that we all like each other and respect each other's privacy."

Roberta's situation is not a common one, nor may it be feasible for many people. Janice, who did not want to move in with her daughter, was expressing a more prevalent opinion. But every set of circumstances is different. Much depends on your own health, as well as the relationship you have with your children. Moreover, you may very well have a variety of other choices open to you:

- Living alone
- Sharing living quarters with a friend—or a friend of a friend

- Advertising for a roommate, or consulting an agency specializing in finding roommates
- Finding a paying boarder to move into an empty room in your home
- Consulting house-sharing organizations that bring together people interested in sharing their homes with other people
- Moving into a resident hotel, or an apartment complex with cardroom, gym facilities, clubhouse, and other social amenities

One woman who lives in one of these complexes with a variety of facilities told us that she can have as much or as little social interaction as she pleases. "Sometimes when I'm feeling a little lonely, but don't really want to do anything, I just sit in the lobby and watch the people go by."

The "Title" of Widowhood

An important point to remember is that the term *widowhood* describes only your *marital position*. It is not a title or a state of mind, nor does it define you as a person. Assuming an aura of "professional widowhood," thinking of yourself primarily as a widow or widower, can impede personal growth and adversely affect emotional and even physical health. It can also add an unnecessary burden to your children's lives.

When Lee's husband died after being bedridden and in and out of hospitals for over a year, she was so prepared for widowhood that she felt as if she was slipping into an old bathrobe.

"I was a widow with my whole heart and soul," said Lee. "Widowhood was my whole life. I made it an excuse for everything I did—and didn't do. And believe me, what I didn't do far surpassed whatever little bit I did.

"I sat in a chair all day, in a stupor, full of self-pity. I

didn't care what I wore, what I looked like. I stopped calling my friends; I didn't want to leave the house.

"I shudder now to think of how I was acting, what I was
doing to myself and my kids, who were leaning over backward to try to make my life enjoyable.

"They were always calling me up, bringing me food,
inviting me out, recommending books for me to read,
movies to see, but there I was, stuck in the deepest kind of
do-nothing rut that anyone could ever dig for herself."

Lee recounted how she finally was able to throw off her
inertia.

"My daughter insisted I come to dinner one night. She
had invited her business colleague, an attractive, lively
woman who was my age. When we were introduced, the
woman smiled and asked me what I do. Without a blink, I
answered, 'Oh, I'm a widow. Two years and three months
now.'

"The woman looked at me and said, 'Really? I didn't
know that *widow* is an occupation.'

"Instantly, I felt my entire insides churn. My poor
daughter jumped right in and changed the subject. I could
see she was devastated.

"At home that night, I took a good look in the mirror
and saw a pale, gaunt, bedraggled woman. 'Two years and
three months,' I said aloud. 'Goodbye, you poor, sad thing.
I don't need you anymore.' "

Lee did not change overnight. A brief look in the mirror will
not give anyone an instant character analysis. Renewing old
friendships and interests, and developing new ones, takes time,
insight, and courage. Self-pity was not the only negative force
imprisoning Lee. She was full of fear, the fear of change.

Fear of change can entwine itself into our lives, choking off
new ideas and actions. If this happens to you, if you feel that

fear is imprisoning you, if you feel stuck in a rut the way Lee was, ask yourself if it is only *change* that you fear. Do you also fear loss of control? You're so comfortable in the old house or apartment, the old way of living, the old ideas. The children live nearby; they're so helpful, so devoted, so loving. Why change, why risk? As everyone knows, life does have risks. We encounter these risks daily, on the job, in the street, on the highway, in the air. If we were to list every potential pitfall, we would never leave the house.

But why dwell on risks? Why concentrate on fear? Lee had allowed her fear to suffocate her and burden her children. Only by recognizing her fear was she finally able to confront it and start to conquer it. Only by being willing to break out of her prison was she able to savor all the wonders of life still open to her.

Are you masking your fear under the guise of grief? After any loss, a grieving period is necessary. But if grief is allowed to sit in your heart, heavy as a stone and just as lifeless and immovable, it will engulf and strangle you in the same way as fear.

If grief is prolonged, if the grieving is not allowed to progress and express itself, if the healing is not allowed to begin, then you are stuck in a grief that probably has ceased to be *grief* and is now *habit*.

Steps in the Healing Process

- Avoid dependence on your children beyond the initial grieving period.
- Avoid using your children to fill the void caused by the death of your spouse.
- Create independent activities for yourself.
- Look for new points of view—see a film you would not ordinarily see; read a book you would not ordinarily read.
- Learn to differentiate between nostalgia and being walled up alive—suffocating from old ways and habits.

- Accept periods of loneliness; devise various ways of dealing with loneliness, including just living with it.

Before you can make a change, you need to accept some parts of the situation. Considering some trade-offs, you may opt for periods of loneliness or financial limitations.

Divorce

Separation as a result of divorce produces many of the same experiences and emotions as does separation by death. Similar decisions often have to be made, and similar steps taken. The same reactions—grief, anger, loneliness, fear of change and of the unknown—may be longer lasting as a result of divorce. Widowhood marks a completion of a phase of life; the effects of divorce can linger for years, tormenting both the spouses and the children.

Death is final; one player has left the game. *Divorce* can be open-ended; the game goes on.

Sometimes parents have remained in a marriage in order to keep the family intact while the children were young. Once the children grow up and become self-sufficient, these parents may decide that their divorce will no longer affect the children. Not so! Be prepared for some negative reactions.

"My daughter was shocked when we told her we were divorcing," said Millie. "After years of being exposed to the fights between my husband and me, I thought she'd agree that this was for the best, but, no, she got excited and said that her life was falling apart. A twenty-five-year-old woman with a loving husband and an adorable baby, and her life was falling apart!

"My husband and I had to soothe her and beg her to understand. It was probably the first time in twenty years that he and I were on the same side."

Millie was prepared for the reality of her divorce, but not for her daughter's reaction. She said afterward that she and her husband had gone about everything in the wrong way, that they should have told their daughter sooner, should have prepared her better. Eventually, the daughter was able to see things in perspective and to admit that the divorce was inevitable, but not before Millie and her husband suffered a lot of guilt and other painful feelings.

Divorce is always a wrenching experience for a family, no matter at what stage it occurs, no matter what the provocation or heartache that precedes it, and no matter if it is carried out in a "civilized" manner or a brutal one. Even when the divorce is a mutual decision, the proceedings themselves can cause anger to surface.

One man described how the reality of divorce caused him to undergo a complete about-face in personality.

> "I never would have believed I'd behave the way I did," said Elliot. "I went into complete hiding for a month. I stayed in a motel room, didn't go to work, wouldn't see my children or anyone else. I isolated myself from the world.
>
> "A whole month! And I was the one who had actively campaigned for the divorce! Boy, did I learn about myself. What I put my children through. My ex-wife, too. It took plenty of time to straighten things out, but now I can thankfully say that my children and I are united again."

Prolonged accusations and bitterness, especially if the children add to the finger-pointing, can stifle any practical considerations and future plans. The children may take sides, or blame the parents equally. Whether you are the parent they are championing or criticizing, by encouraging communication, forgiveness, and completion, you will be helping to ease a difficult situation.

At such an upsetting time, the family unit needs to adopt constructive attitudes, in order for its members to create and maintain a sense of "belonging."

Help Yourself and Your Children

- If you are the initiating party, minimize feeling guilty; avoid feeling that you have to explain your actions.
- Encourage your children to understand and forgive both parents.
- Help your children to know that you will work to make your new situation easier for them than your previous one.

Avoid a Rift Between You and Your Children

Many parents undergoing a divorce suffer the same kind of reaction from their children that Jack did after his wife died. Jack's children accused him of neglect. During divorce proceedings, many children may make similar accusations.

By acknowledging the children's feelings, and talking to them honestly and with patience and understanding, you can help to minimize the hard feelings, the sadness, and the pain.

- Acknowledge the pain brought about by the divorce.
- Avoid criticizing—or vilifying—your ex-spouse.
- Avoid too much dependence on your children.

Remarriage

When deciding to remarry, feel fortunate if your children immediately and wholeheartedly applaud your plans. Do not be surprised, however, if they object. One man was taken aback by his children's response to his announcement that he was remarrying: "Really, Dad! Act your age!" Hurt and disappointed, he decided to keep his feelings to himself and gave a lighthearted and flippant reply: "So maybe I'm not acting my age. So what? Listen, kids, you only live once. Don't you want your dear old dad to have one last fling in his old age?" To his relief, both his son and daughter laughed and wished him luck. The father, although happy with the outcome, had been prepared in any case to go ahead with his wedding plans, even if his children had not been supportive.

Whichever way you communicate with your children, emphasize your love for them and your desire that they continue to be an integral part of your life—while you also spin off into your own newly created "space."

What Are Your Children's Concerns?

- Finances and inheritance
- Fear of alienation of affection—fear that you will give all your love to your new mate
- Anger at the parent who initiated the divorce
- Anger at the parent who wants to remarry
- Disloyalty or guilt toward the replaced parent or toward the memory of the deceased parent
- Guilt at being happy with the new step-parent
- Dislike of the prospective mate
- Competition with the children of the prospective mate

Pave the Way to Get What You Want: A Happy Remarriage and a Loving Relationship With Your Children

- Encourage communication between all involved.
- Listen to the children's concerns, without needing to defend your actions or intentions.
- Reassure them of your own feelings of love and consideration.
- Evaluate any guilt they may try to make you feel, or that you may feel yourself.
- Keep your sense of humor.
- Avoid becoming defensive.

Reorganize Your Family Life

Remarriage involves more than a marriage between two people. Two families are involved. The other children may have been raised differently from yours. Your new mate may have different expectations for his children than you do for yours. Although you will be interacting with the new family and will be giving them a certain amount of attention, you cannot become an "instant parent." Do not expect your spouse's adult children to be similar to your adult children or to want intimacy with you.

Allotting time for the children and grandchildren of the new spouse requires some thought. Study the new situation. Geographic distance separating the members of the family may make frequent visits impractical. Telephone calls, chatty letters, greeting cards, and little gifts for the grandchildren are effective distance-breakers. Keep in mind, however, the family style of your new spouse. Every family is different; every family has its own style of communicating, showing affection, and giving gifts. Those styles should be respected.

If the new family is open and friendly, and encourages interaction, take that as your cue. If, on the other hand, the family is reserved or not interested in too many overtures, again act accordingly. Discussing these matters with your new spouse and observing the way he or she acts will help you to learn how to deal with the membersof your new family.

Before deciding to remarry, you may be facing some challenges and decisions.

In one instance, the future wife's adult son lived with her. Her future husband was uncertain about what he should say or do.

"I thought about it a lot," said Arnold. "Nancy's son, Jay, was a nice boy. But that was the whole point. There he was, thirty-two, and still a *boy*. He had a good job but no gumption, no drive.

"I didn't know what to do. I sure didn't want to lose Nancy, and she didn't want to throw Jay out.

"In the end, I decided to buy the whole package. I moved into Nancy's house, complete with Jay. It wasn't the best arrangement, but it wasn't too bad. And Jay and I became rather close.

"But I did have some explaining to do to my own children, and some hurt feelings to soothe. Anyway, it lasted only two years. Jay's on his own now, and everything's smoothed out."

On the other side of this coin, the parent of the adult child still living at home has to decide whether to keep the situation as it is and try to persuade the new mate to accept it, or to encourage the adult child to become more independent.

Another point to consider is the interaction between the adult children of both families. You and your new spouse may want your adult children to share frequent social occasions. If both sides agree, fine; if one side does not wish to have too much involvement, that's fine, too. It is important for the parents not to insist that the children of the two families be close. One set of adult children may be considerably older or younger than the other, or have a different lifestyle, all of which could widen the gap between them.

- Keep in mind that two separate families are involved.
- Set aside time for both families.
- Integrate the two families as much or as little as is desired.
- Avoid pushing or hurrying the relationship.
- Avoid insisting that the children of both families be close.
- Avoid criticizing one set of children to another.

Single Status

The meaning of the word *single* has changed in the last twenty or so years. Formerly meaning not *yet* married, today the word means not *now* married.

For many, single status lifestyle is a choice. How we carry out this choice is a reflection of our fantasies, material means, and cultural and familial conditioning.

- How much will you be inhibited by the watchful eyes of others?
- How often do you hear these words from your adult child?
  "Mom, your skirt is too short."
  "Dad, that woman you brought to dinner is younger than I am."

How dependent or independent are you? In what ways? Are you comfortable with this situation?

How Do Your Children Feel About Your Independence?

- Do they admire your independence?
- Do they worry about your physical well-being and tell you that you should not drive so much, or live alone?
- Are they disappointed if you don't have too much time to spend with them or their children?
- Are they upset that you are dating?

How Do Your Children Feel About Your Dependence?

- Do they resent your dependence?
- Do they encourage your dependence?
- Do they worry about your physical well-being, that you're not eating properly or otherwise taking care of yourself?
- Are they distressed if you're unwilling or unable to make decisions?
- Do they resent it when you ask them to pay your bills, handle your daily chores, or take care of your household repairs?

Reorganize Your Life, Your Attitudes,
and Your Concept of Yourself

- Realize what you can and cannot do.

- Recognize that independence does not always have to take the form of action; it can also be a state of mind—an optimistic, upbeat attitude.
- Recognize when you need assistance.
- Consider assistance from sources other than your children.
- Be aware of your needs and desires, and of how they can affect your children.

New Habits . . . New Hobbies . . . New Freedom . . . New You

What if your children do not want a new you; what if they just want dear old Mom or dear old Dad? Think about the concept of letting go. It works both ways! Discuss this concept with your children in a candid way, remaining as unemotional as possible. Explain your situation, your needs and desires; talk about their lives, their needs and desires.

One woman who had a serious relationship with a man, but who was not interested in marrying him, was confronted with her children's disapproval.

"My son and daughter were very upset with me," said Celeste. "They told me over and over that I was acting contrary to my character. They told me that my living with a man not my husband caused them a lot of embarrassment.

"I didn't know what to do. I didn't want to tell my children to mind their own business, but I also didn't want them to be uncomfortable and embarrassed. Above all, I had no wish to marry again.

"So what did I do? Nothing. I listened to them without comment. I didn't argue, didn't try to change their opinions, didn't try to explain mine. I did tell them that although I didn't agree with them, I respected their opinions. I also told them that I loved them and hoped that things would turn out for the best.

"The kids eventually got used to the idea. They always liked my friend, Hank, and now they've learned to accept the situation."

By following her own instincts and desires, Celeste was able to live the way she wanted. Her lifestyle was contrary to her children's wishes, but because she neither ridiculed them nor tried to change their minds, she was able to keep their goodwill and their love.

At this time of life, your sense of self may very well become stronger. Your own unique preferences may help you to shape a way of life that *you* want, undeterred by the rules or wishes of others.

Life is always in a state of flux. We change; our circumstances change; our needs change. How we adjust to these changes, how we maintain satisfying relationships with our adult children, and how we strive to fulfill our own needs will help determine the quality of our lives.

We often need a combination of closeness and aloneness. Periods of *voluntary aloneness*—as opposed to *loneliness*—can lighten the mind and rejuvenate the spirit. You don't have to sit in your room by yourself, thinking and brooding. You can walk on city streets or country roads, you can visit museums, you can listen to music, you can go to a film or a play. These are healing activities, indulged in equally well with people or alone.

One man described how he found solace after the death of his wife.

"I was surrounded by my children and my friends. They were all so good to me, but there were times when I just couldn't face anyone.

"One afternoon, I took my granddaughter out for a walk in the park. She was five at the time. We talked, and we were silent. The companionship, the closeness, the warmth of her little hand in mine, gave me a feeling of peace, and something else—a feeling of continuity.

"There I was with my granddaughter. She was my wife's granddaughter, too, and suddenly I felt my wife's presence between us. It was almost as if she were walking with us."

We draw strength from many sources—ourselves, our family and friends, books, art, music. All of these have the power to delight and to heal.

Exercise

1. Create a picture album.
   - See the different stages of life and the shifts in your involvements.
   - Create a pictorial time-line with photos that will reflect the different stages and involvement, and where the focus was in your life.
   - Where is the focus now?
   - Which photo would you like to choose for your life now?
2. Shift your focus from the family; step outside the family unit.
   - List the ways you are already on the way—your activities separate from the family.
   - List what you are planning to do, what you want to do.
   - List the ways you are still connected, or the ways you keep coming back to be connected.
   - List the activities you share with your family.
   - What family activities may be created for the future?

Chapter 11

Beyond Parenting: Creating New Visions

 "Who am I now?"
"Where would I like to be a year from now?"
"What do I have to do to get there?"

Suddenly you are like a youngster in a store—but instead of toys displayed before you, there are choices of attitude and choices of lifestyle. Check your perception of life. Is the glass half full or half empty? Is the sky partly sunny or partly cloudy? Are you ready to start a new chapter in your life?

Asking yourself these questions allows you to separate from the past, examine the present, and plan for the future. Thinking about them frees you to view this stage of life as an opportunity to expand your horizons.

Raising young children was a major focus in many parents' lives; for others, this was less so. In any case, shedding and outgrowing the specific responsibilities of active parenting can leave a space in your life, and you may be uncomfortable with this space. Empty time is like an empty closet: somehow it fills itself up. Before you can blink an eye, both your time and your life can be filled in a haphazard fashion. It's so easy to let this happen, so easy to just "float" along. With all the opportunities available, it's just as easy to fill your life with your own personal preferences. *Consciously electing* to organize and design your time—by adding new interests, dropping old ones, and keeping others—will be more satisfying than if you just drift along and let everything "grow like Topsy." Whatever you decide to have in your life will be of your choosing.

After so many years spent taking care of young children, even if you have learned to let go, even if you fully accept the fact of your children's mature, independent status, you may still find yourself somewhat at loose ends. You may feel a little tentative, a little lost or insecure.

And even when you are fully on track, there may be times when you forget that you're no longer engaged in active parenting. Most people can relate to Greta's story.

> "I was in the supermarket, picking out peaches," said Greta, mother of two married children. "All of a sudden I heard a little boy yell, 'Ma!' In a flash, I dropped the peaches, whirled around, and called out, 'Here I am, honey, over here!' "

Greta went on to describe how she felt afterward.

> "I laughed when I thought about it later, but I cringed a little, too. I found myself actually praying that I won't get to be like my brother and sister-in-law who think and talk about nothing but their kids. Both children are over thirty, but to listen to the way their parents carry on, you'd swear the kids were still in diapers."

We all know people like Greta's brother and sister-in-law. Although on the surface they may acknowledge their children's adult status, they still have not let go in spirit. Their conversations are constantly peppered with stories of their children's circumstances and activities. When their children were very young, these parents droned on about baby food and toilet training; then came endless recountings of grade school, summer camp, and college.

Now, these parents chatter about their children's apartments in the city, their children's houses in the suburbs, their children's boyfriends and girlfriends, their children's live-in mates, their children's marriage plans (or lack of them). On and on, they prattle about their children; on and on, goes the vicarious thrill, until some of their friends want to scream, "Isn't it about time you got yourself a life of your own?"

Aside from burdening friends and relatives with stories about their children's exploits, conquests, or foibles, some parents burden themselves and their children with needless worry. It is understandable to look back wistfully and remember the evenings when the children were small, at home, and safe in their beds.

We may think that we're ready to adopt a new focus in our lives, but it is hard to embark on the new course.

Dennis told us that he was in a state of perpetual worry.

> "I was never this nervous when the kids were small. Lately, I can't stop thinking about them. They're doing all right, but I keep imagining them losing their jobs, their houses burning down, their airplanes crashing—all kinds of disasters happening."

A little probing brought forth the information that Dennis had been retired for about a year. A man of no hobbies or interests, he had transferred the energy that had been spent on his business career to worrying about his children. He was using worry to fill his otherwise empty life.

Worrying can become an obsession, an indulgence, masking a secret desire for control. Dennis was deluding himself into thinking that he was continuing his role as an active parent. Actually, he burdened his children with his constant expressions of concern.

By now you are accustomed to the idea of letting go. More

than a concept, letting go is a process, a gradual one, full of fits and starts. It can be looked upon as a journey that a parent has to take. As with any journey, you start with some general suggestions, hone them down, and set an itinerary of your own. The journey is full of challenge and growth, and so is this time of life. You are moving toward a new style of interaction with your children and a new stage of discovery for yourself. Now is the time to re-focus and reorganize your life.

It is proper—it is desirable—it is wonderful!—for your children to share a part of your lives. But what part, and how much?

Interacting With Adult Children: When, How, How Much?

There are parents who forget or who cannot face the reality that their children are grown and independent; there are adult children who put their parents into a stereotyped mold of the loving, willing caregiver who is always there and always on call.

An important shift in parenting has taken place. Loving and nurturing are still vital parts of the parent-child relationship, but the proportion is different. Both generations are now independent and adult. Neither generation can think for the other, speak for the other, monopolize the other, or take the other for granted.

Your adult children now occupy part of your "social time." It can be fun to talk with them, fun to visit with them, and fun to go places with them. But, as with most human relationships, some degree of planning or structuring is helpful. You want to spend time with your children without having to suspend or surrender the other parts of your life.

Many parents describe certain "situations" that tend to complicate their lives.

"It happens so often. We think we have a free weekend, and then all of a sudden, a car pulls up—and there they are."

"I thought I'd have lots of time for my old friends, and

time to make new ones, but I seem to be busier than ever with my family."

"I don't get to see the kids except on weekends. And when they come, they are couples. We become a crowd. There are times when I yearn to have a few private words with one or another of them as individuals."

"We love having our children over. We enjoy their company and have great stimulating conversations—but I always end up exhausted. I'm busy planning and cooking meals. *Adult* meals. It's not like the old days when they were little. I can't get away with peanut butter anymore!"

Smoothing out such "situations" requires understanding, tact, and planning.

- Share your calendar with your children to avoid conflicts between their visits and your other activities.
- If you have to disappoint your children, suggest an alternate time.
- Keep in mind the big picture. Sometimes, in order to consider the best interests of all, you may be willing to compromise, to have things not quite the way you would have chosen.
- Keep in mind also that there are times when you have to be brave enough to say "no."
- Be ready to learn from each experience how to make the next one even better.
- Be receptive to spontaneous get-togethers. You wouldn't want to miss some unexpected fun. *Carpe diem*—embrace the day!

When the children were young, your time was taken up with supervising homework, health, clothes, Little League, piano lessons, and the like. You could put it all in place and plan recreation time for yourself. Now your children have their own schedules. Arranging time with them requires the same consideration you give to arranging time with your friends. Having time for everything requires some thought, but can bring big rewards. Recreational contacts with your children are possible in many areas—depending upon your preferences, skills, hobbies, or new interests that you would like to add to your life. Do you and your children play tennis? A good game of doubles may be very satisfying. Listening to music ("yours" and "theirs") is another way to share time.

Controlling Your Own Time and Energy

We cannot always expect our children to spend a set amount of time with us. The parents may have extra free time, but their children may not. Or the reverse may be true. Perhaps both sides have business or social interests that prevent them from being readily available. In any case, command appearances serve no one.

Similarly, children cannot always expect their parents to be accessible. What if you're presented with a dilemma—who do you spend time with, your friends or your children? If there is a conflict, how do you resolve the situation?

Possible solutions:

- Honor your first commitment unless extraordinary circumstances dictate otherwise.
- Be considerate of and sensitive to your child's feelings.
    Refuse, if you must, in a positive but gentle way.
    Suggest another time.
- In your planning, aim for balance—time to spend with your children and time to spend with your friends.

See yourself as separate from your children. Remember, you are neither abandoning nor "divorcing" them. But your children are not your hobby. Increasing your contact with friends—old and new, people of your own age and stage of life, or people older or younger, but people *unconnected* with your children—will broaden your interests.

Sometimes, what starts out as a pleasurable experience can turn into a chore. Sara was able to break what had become an inconvenient and tiresome ritual.

> "Al and I set up a bridge game with our daughter and son-in-law," Sara told us. "We started out playing once in a while but, before we knew it, we had a game every Wednesday night.
>
> "It was lovely at first, but soon it became an obligation—on both sides. We began to notice that the kids kept begging off with a different excuse each time. There were times when we wanted to beg off, too, but didn't.
>
> "Finally, we decided to be candid with the children. I suggested to them that we be more flexible. We've adopted a sort of 'catch-as-catch-can' policy. It's worked out fine. The pressure is off."

If overdone, any ritual, no matter how delightful in the beginning, can become burdensome. Flexibility brings better results.

What Now, for Me? Planning Your Life

So, you've let go—or at least you're working on it. You may be asking yourself, "What now, for me?" Adding new elements to your life will help you find the answer.

A good way to begin is to review the questions that opened this chapter:

"Who am I *now*?"
"Where would I like to be a year from now?"
"What do I have to do to get there?"

1. *"Who am I now?"*

   What is the first role that comes to mind when you describe yourself? Parent? Spouse? Businessperson? Are you satisfied with this assessment? Would you like a change?

2. *Where would I like to be a year from now?"*

   Maybe the answer is a complicated one. Sort it out. Pick a goal. Is it realistic? Achievable? If not, you can modify it into one that *is* achievable.

3. *What do I have to do to get there?"*

   Write down what you have chosen as your new goal. Think about how it can be achieved. It may not be reached in one giant step. Divide the process into a series of easy steps and stages.

Getting What You Want: Practical Matters

The natural successor to the question, "What now, for me?" is "Why not?" Why not study French? Why not move to the city? Why not move to the country? Why not travel to the Orient?

The world is full of ideas and possibilities. Instead of avoiding them or pushing them away because they are new to you, use your experience and eagerness to help you explore them. Think of the possibilities. Try some of them. Not all will work. Try others. This attitude will keep you vibrant and active, and participating in the present.

Be realistic, financially and logistically, but also let your imagination run free. Although no one can have everything, it is equally true that you can have much of what you want.

Remember the dreams of your youth? Do you still yearn for them? Try to make part of those dreams come true.

- You always wanted to play the piano? Find a piano teacher, or take a book from the library on piano lessons, self-taught.

- You always wanted to sing with a band? Sing with a glee club, a church choir, or a community group. (If nobody can stand to listen to you, sing in the shower!)
- You wanted to be a doctor? What is there about it that appeals to you? The medical setting? Healing and helping? Perhaps volunteer work in a hospital would bring you joy.
- You never had enough time to read the classics? Sign up for a "great books" course at a local school or library.
- You would like to try your hand in politics? Contact your local party organization.
- You are concerned about the environment? Call one of the many organizations involved.

Think also of art, cooking, crafts, physical fitness, volunteer work. Think of any field you would like to explore. Ideas and projects can be found everywhere.

Maybe you like exactly what you have been doing. You now have time to do more of it!

A word of caution: Do not feel pressured. Do not feel that you must do something—either because others are doing it, or because it's a prestigious thing to do, or because you have already started it. Give yourself permission to stop a project in midair.

From a rather unlikely beginning, Willis found a whole new lifestyle. He told us that all he started out to do was lose some weight.

"I figured if I really tried I could drop fifteen pounds," said Willis. "Right after I started my diet, I saw a television program about nutrition. The next day, I took some books from the library and, before I knew it, I was hooked. I changed my entire way of eating, joined a gym, and lost twenty-five pounds.

"But the important thing is that I actually find my new regimen exciting. It's like getting a new hobby.

"And I met some great people at the gym. My children can't get over the change. They say I'm a new person."

If all of this sounds just a little too Pollyannaish, we can mention the other side of life.

True, life is full of change, some of it not so good, not so pleasant, and not so comfortable. You may have to confront the loss of your youth. You may have to confront the loss of your health, your mate, and close family members and friends. But, although you may be dealing with personal losses and an aging body, you can aim for a vigorous mind. The body is like an old car. It has to be taken to the repair shop every now and then, but if you think of it as a vintage Rolls-Royce, life can become more precious with age. The mind, when you're lucky—and when you give it a chance—can be resilient and strong. The more you use it, the better it can work for you.

If possible, do not let poor health or other setbacks rule your life. Keeping busy usually makes one feel better. Everyone has some kind of ache, pain, or condition. Within your own limits and your own inclinations, schedule a full life for yourself.

Use your skills to restructure your life. If you focus your attention on your limitations, they will overwhelm you. Focus, instead, on your skills and strengths—and your new goals.

Implementing Your New Plans: Wider Horizons

It takes imagination, energy, and, yes, courage to lift up your head from an established lifestyle and engage in something new. It may or may not be something you share with your friends or your mate, but if it is important to you, don't give it up.

How do you get started? Whether you do something alone or with friends, develop a campaign of action.

Several people told us that they forged new lives for themselves in a deliberate way—with lists of choices and lists of the steps to take.

Some people mentioned making "contracts" with themselves. They write down what they want to do, and then give themselves dates to start.

One woman called her method "taking the plunge."

"I've always loved astronomy," said Martha. "I spend a good deal of my vacations in planetariums. One day, I heard of an astronomy club about fifty miles away. I really wanted to look into it, but I hesitated. Here I am, a single woman, living alone. The meetings are at night—to view the stars through a telescope—and they are about an hour's drive away. Also, the thought of not knowing anyone, of just barging in there, made me uneasy.

"I decided to list all the pros and cons of joining. I started with the cons and filled up the page. I felt awful. Then I turned to the pro column, but all I could write was, 'I love astronomy. I want to join the club.' I sat there and finally I wrote it again, this time in capital letters: 'I LOVE ASTRONOMY. I WANT TO JOIN THE CLUB.'

"That was that. I still remember the way I felt when I went to the first meeting. It was intoxicating! I've felt that way ever since."

Martha used "intoxicating" to describe her feelings. Another way of putting it is, "wonderful"—"full of wonder." What an apt description for this stage of our lives: full of wonder, full of challenge, full of potential for personal growth.

Points to remember:

- Enjoy the big world out there. It can be fascinating.
- Plan—choose—what you want for something new in your life, whether others approve or not. You are past the "what will people think" stage. Do what works for *you*.
- Offer to share your interests with your spouse or friends, but do not be discouraged if your offer is refused.

Positive results of an independent life:

- New, interesting use of time and energy
- Increased self-esteem
- "Benign neglect" of your children, freeing both you and them from guilt, and freeing you for your own pursuits

Do not let this stage of your life be merely a "winding down" or a giving up.

Staying on Target: Maintaining Your Goals

As part of the "sandwich generation," many of us are involved with the care of our own parents. As you focus on your own goals, be willing to divert your energy—temporarily—to any urgent needs of your aging parents or your adult children. Participating in family life can help you to satisfy your perception of yourself, maintain your sense of integrity, and express your love and support for your loved ones. All the while, however, remain cognizant of your personal desires. Return on track as soon as possible.

Parents of grown children do not speak with one voice. We are not one group, not one age, not one specific generation. We may be in our forties, fifties, sixties, seventies, or older. We may be married or single. We may be employed or retired. What we all have in common is that our children are now adults. They fly from the nest, and so, in a sense, can we.

Carpe diem—embrace the day!

- Adorn it with riches of yesterday.
- Brighten it with hopes for tomorrow.
- Enjoy it with blessings of the present.

Reflection

Think of your friends who are older than you. Think of those whose lifestyles or interests you see as admirable. Which of their activities would you like to engage in?

Exercises

1. Daydream. Pretend you have a new life. Choose any skills and strengths you would like to have.
2. Make a list of the things you have thought about wanting to do but never had the time or opportunity when the children were small. Which of these can you choose to do now? What steps must you take to achieve your goals?
3. Write a contract with yourself that states your new goals and the course of action needed to achieve them. Set a time-line for satisfying the contract.
4. Review the questions:
   - Who am I now?
   - Who would I like to be? Now? A year from now? Five years from now?
   - How do I achieve these goals?

Start your preparation for the next decade now. Living is a process.

Suggested Readings

Ashner, Laurie, and Meyerson, Mitch. *When Parents Love Too Much*. New York: William Morrow, 1990.

Becnel, Barbara. *The Co-Dependent Parent; Free Yourself By Freeing Your Child*. Los Angeles: Lowell House, 1990.

Dodson, Dr. Fitzhugh, with Paula Reuben. *How to Grandparent*. New York: Harper & Row, 1981.

Greene, A. L., and Boxer, Andrew M. *Daughters and Sons As Young Adults: Restructuring the Ties That Bind*. Hillsdale, New Jersey: Lawrence Erlbaum Associates, 1986.

Haines, James, and Neely, Margery. *Parents' Work Is Never Done*. Far Hills, New Jersey: New Horizon Press, 1987.

Johnson, Colleen Leahy. *Ex Familia: Grandparents, Parents, and Children Adjust To Divorce*. New Brunswick, New Jersey: Rutgers University Press, 1988.

Klingelhofer, Edwin L. *Coping With Your Grown Children*. Clifton, New Jersey: Humana Press, Inc., 1989.

Kornhaber, Arthur. *Between Parents and Grandparents*. New York: St. Martin's Press, 1986.

Okimoto, Jean Davies, and Stegall, Phyllis Jackson. *Boomerang Kids*. New York: Pocket Books, 1989.